DOCTOR AT NAGASAKI

DOCTOR AT NAGASAKI

"My First Assignment Was Mercy Killing"

by Masao Shiotsuki

Kōsei Publishing Co. · *Tokyo*

The photograph on the cover of an atomic bomb victim of
Nagasaki, a fourteen-year-old girl brought to Omura Naval
Hospital, was taken by the author on August 10 or 11, 1945.

This book was originally published in Japanese under the title *Hatsushigoto wa
Anrakusatsu datta*.

Translated by Simul International, Inc.

Cover design by Nobu Miyazaki. The text of this book is set in a computer version of Baskerville with a computer version of Optima for display.

First English Edition, 1987

Published by Kōsei Publishing Co., Kōsei Building, 2-7-1
Wada, Suginami-ku, Tokyo 166. Copyright © 1987 by Kōsei
Publishing Co.; all rights reserved. Printed in Japan.

ISBN 4-333-01250-3   LCC Card No. applied for

CONTENTS

FOREWORD

When the atomic bomb was dropped on Nagasaki on August 9, 1945, I was a doctor at a small, very modestly equipped tuberculosis sanatorium run by the Catholic church that was located on the high ground of Urakami, 1,400 meters from the hypocenter. It was a clear day. The air raid sirens had sounded once, but since no enemy planes made their appearance, the alert was finally called off. Just as I thought that we had been spared an attack that day, an incredibly bright light flashed over the sanatorium. From that instant began a string of days and nights during which I was surrounded, in that completely burned out sanatorium, by the critically wounded and the dead.

The Japanese army and navy were both by that time nearly powerless and most of the major cities of Japan had been reduced to ashes in heavy incendiary bombing. On August 6, an atomic bomb had been dropped on Hiroshima and the city had been totally destroyed. Although Japan's defeat was clear and inevitable, the military had chosen to lead the people blindly to utter destruction.

When the atomic bomb was dropped on Nagasaki, Dr. Shiotsuki was an idealistic and earnest young doctor at Omura Naval Hospital, 20 kilometers northeast of the city. When the Pacific War began, all Japanese medical talent was drafted into the military. Omura Naval Hospital was built with an eye for the expected expansion of the war and it was the pride of the imperial navy, with the latest in equipment and the most highly qualified personnel.

When the plutonium-fueled atomic bomb exploded in the sky 500 meters above Matsuyama-machi, in the northwest sector of Nagasaki, it created an enormous blast of wind that destroyed buildings and threw people about. This was accompanied by a heat of several tens of thousands of degrees that incinerated people and their homes, and also by a great amount of life-destroying radiation.

Near the center of the city as I was (in contrast to Dr. Shiotsuki), I was confronted immediately after the blast with a horrible sight: people with their skulls cracked open by the blast, children with their stomach walls torn open leaving their intestines exposed, and others covered with blood after being pierced all over their bodies with fragments of glass and splinters of wood driven into them by the force of the bomb's explosion. These and others like them had managed to totter and crawl to the yard of our sanatorium, only to collapse there. The glass and wood fragments had been blown deep into their bodies, even penetrating their internal organs. Some had fallen under collapsing homes or walls and been burned black underneath the flaming rubble; even those who somehow managed to escape burning to death under roof tiles or other materials and had escaped from the inferno suffered broken bones and spinal contusions and were unable to walk. Some had their limbs severed in the blast or the destruction that followed. There was nothing we could do for any of them.

The Nagasaki Medical College Hospital, the major medical facility in the area, was located only 600 meters from the hypocenter and had collapsed, producing a great number of casualties. As a result, no treatment was available to most of the atomic bomb victims. Relief squads arrived in the city from other parts of the prefecture and other prefectures, and they set up temporary headquarters in elementary schools throughout the city that had escaped destruction. Though they did their best to offer treatment to the victims, they were overwhelmed by the number of patients and the severity of their injuries.

As that long hot summer day in Nagasaki came to an end, a number of these atomic bomb victims finally arrived at Omura Naval Hospital, after a thirty-kilometer train journey. By the time they reached the hospital, many were barely recognizable as human beings. The hospital, after receiving more than seven hundred bomb victims in the short space of one night, had been transformed into a nightmarish condition, and Dr. Shiotsuki applied himself to the treatment of the victims, a task which he persevered at for several days and nights, without sleep. But there was no treatment he could offer his patients, either. In the end, the best he could do was inject them with morphine and provide them a few moments of relief from their pain as he helplessly watched them die. This helplessness, which forced him repeatedly into the role of a mercy killer, continued to haunt Dr. Shiotsuki until his death in 1979.

Almost no one in Japan at that time knew that the "new type of bomb" that had been dropped on Hiroshima and Nagasaki in turn was an atomic weapon. And even if they had known this, no one could have imagined the effects of the radiation that the bomb released.

Four or five days after the bombing, while the surviving patients were still being treated, the hair of patients who had suffered relatively light injuries began to fall out at the lightest touch. Purple spots began to appear on their skin, accompanied by bleeding and bloody discharges. Eventually the purple blotches spread over the entire body and the patient died. These symptoms—the marks of acute radiation poisoning—began to appear on one patient after another, and they struck fear in both Dr. Shiotsuki and myself. In my sanatorium at Urakami, the circle of the dead spread out like a ripple, claiming ever larger numbers of patients; at Omura, the results were the same.

The symptoms of acute radiation poisoning remained in evidence for approximately two weeks. But the effects of radiation did not end there, and within two to five weeks after the bombing, the symptoms of subacute radiation poisoning appeared. By this time a certain degree of treatment and investigation had become possible, and we were beginning to realize that the radiation had destroyed the blood-producing mechanisms of the body. Many continued to die after experiencing epilation, bleeding at the gums, oral lesions, bloody stools, subcutaneous hemorrhaging, and anemia; but some who also showed these symptoms and expected death to claim them survived. Those living near the sanatorium belonged to this group, and the clinic marked a sort of border between life and death: those who had been closer to the center of the explosion died and those farther were saved. I felt as if I resided at the boundary between this world and the next as I sat in the sanatorium surrounded by the bomb's victims.

From five weeks to eight weeks after the bombing, the symptoms of subchronic radiation poisoning began to appear. Though its victims suffered from epilation, oral lesions, and bloody discharges, most survived. Yet they remained far from cured.

One of the greatest cruelties of radiation poisoning is that victims may seem to recover or at first not even show symptoms of affliction, only to suffer from the disease at a later point. This forces the victims to live in constant fear and anxiety. Among the symptoms that may eventually occur are keloids, genital disorders, congenital disorders in infants exposed to radiation while in the womb, optic and blood disorders, and malignant tumors.

Keloids are ugly raised scars. They form on wounds

on the eyelids, ears, lips, hands, and palms, leaving adhesions, contractions, and functional disabilities. They are particularly tragic marks of the bombing for young men and women to bear. Disorders of the genitals result in sterility, miscarriages, and stillbirths. A number of infants in utero whose mothers were near to the center of the explosion have been born with microcephaly and cardiac disease; this was another unexpected result of the bombing that could not be known at the time. Optical disorders in the form of cataracts began to occur with great frequency five to ten years after the bombing. Leukemia is one blood disorder related to the bombing. A peak of leukemia cases among bomb victims occurred five to seven years after the event. Another is aplastic anemia. It has now been proven that exposure to radiation is a cause of malignant tumors, and atomic bomb victims have a greater chance of developing thyroid, lung, and ovary cancer. In addition, bomb victims age more quickly than normal, and it is impossible to dismiss the possibility of hereditary influences that they may pass on to their children and grandchildren.

As one of the major policies of General Douglas MacArthur's occupation, Japan was placed under a press code. The reasons for this were to preserve the peace under the allied occupation and to protect military security and the secrets of the atomic bomb. The occupation was afraid of the criticism that would be directed at the United States if the story of the tremendous cruelty of the atomic bomb were to become known in Japan and throughout the world. The murder of so many civilians, without warning and without discrimination, was a wound on the conscience of the United States, whatever official defense they gave for the bombs' use. Any mention of the atomic bomb was prohibited, not only in the channels of mass communication such as newspapers and magazines, but also in works of literature, such as novels and poems. The Japanese people had been denied freedom of expression during the war by the military establishment; after the war, for a period of seven years, they were prohibited to speak of the atomic bombing by the U.S. occupation. This enforced silence contributed to a forgetting of the terrible impact of the atomic bomb.

But even under the restrictions of the press code, the scientific investigation of the effects of the atomic bombing was designated as the most important task of the United States Commission for the Atomic Bomb Survey. A group of American and Japanese scholars in the fields of physics, biology, and medicine investigated the results of the bombings of Hiroshima and Nagasaki and published their findings, through the auspices of the Japan Society for the Promotion of Science, in 1951 under the title *Genshi Bakudan Saigai Chosa Hokokusho* (Report on the Investigation into Atomic Bomb Damage). The group was recognized for the high quality and broad scale of its efforts, and their report was authoritative.

Yet Dr. Shiotsuki and I, and others who had witnessed the scene of the bombing and its victims soon after the event, couldn't help but feel there were several problems with the report. First, the investigation began forty days after the bombing of Nagasaki. By that time over 90 percent of the victims who were to die of acute injuries caused by the blast, thermal rays, and radiation were already dead. At the same time, the frightening aftereffects of radiation had not yet begun to make themselves known. Then, too, the investigation was carried out under the leadership of the occupying forces, and, the atomic bomb victims were citizens of a defeated nation. Even when the objective nature of the report as an unemotional scientific description of the results of the bombings is taken into consideration, the victims often seemed to be regarded, whether intentionally or not, as experimental subjects rather than human beings. More patently outlandish statements were made by some American scientists, among them the suggestion that the great number of casualties and their seriousness was somehow linked to Japanese physiology, and, at a time when the long-term aftereffects of the bombings were beginning to appear with ever greater frequency, the claim that the damage wrought by the atomic bomb had come to an end.

In 1952, an International Conference of Medical Practitioners was scheduled to convene in Italy, and Dr. Shiotsuki was preparing to present information on the atomic bomb there. The presentation was to include his own valuable testimony concerning his experiences in treating victims of radiation poisoning, the report on atomic bomb damage mentioned above, and data collected on the bomb victims of Hiroshima by Professor Shun'ichi Mashimo of Kyoto University.

Dr. Shiotsuki hoped to show the doctors of the world that medicine was powerless in the face of the great number of casualties produced by the atomic bomb and the deadly effects of radiation poisoning.

But at the last minute this purely medical and humanitarian conviction to spread information about the effects of the atomic bomb fell victim to Cold War politics. Pressure from certain sources prevented the reports on atomic bomb victims from finding a forum in the international scientific community and, indeed, the conference itself was canceled immediately before it was to convene. The relationship between the United States and the Soviet Union was at that time extremely tense. No longer was America the sole proprietor of the atomic bomb. The hydrogen bomb had been developed and the nuclear arms race was proceeding at full speed. The Soviet military establishment, at the same time it was developing atomic weapons, was attempting to use the American bombing of Japan for propaganda purposes. Thus it was that Japan lost its chance to present the results of the atomic bombings, even to an international medical conference. Dr. Shiotsuki's efforts finally bore fruit, however, thirty years later, with the formation of the International Physicians for the Prevention of Nuclear War (IPPNW).

The IPPNW is an international medical association founded by Dr. Bernard Lown, a professor at the Harvard School of Public Health, and Dr. Yevgeni Chazov, director of the USSR Cardiological Institute, in 1980. The headquarters are in Boston. Over

150,000 doctors from forty-nine countries are members. In Japan alone 2,400 doctors belong to the group.

The members of the IPPNW are dedicated to preventing nuclear war "as a consequence of their professional commitments to protect life and preserve health." One of their duties is to circulate information about the consequences of nuclear war throughout the world. They refrain, however, in the course of these activities, from taking a stand on any specific policy of any government. With the establishment of the IPPNW, the medical profession, which bears most directly the responsibility for humanity's health and life, has joined together to oppose nuclear war, because at last doctors have come to realize the acute threat to human survival those weapons represent. Better late than never.

Science has progressed to the stage where it has developed nuclear weapons, a tool to destroy humanity altogether. In the forty years since the first use of those weapons on Hiroshima and Nagasaki, their total energy yield has grown more than a millionfold, until they fill the sky above us, the land, and the seas. If they are ever used again, they will claim an unimaginable number of instantaneous victims, and many, many more will suffer from radiation poisoning—a number so great as to dwarf the number of Japanese victims of the bombs. Medical facilities will be destroyed and many doctors will die as well. It is important to bring home the message to all humanity that there is no medical solution to nor even medical relief from the effects of nuclear weapons.

The true and fundamental wish of all on earth, the total elimination of nuclear arms, is on the verge of becoming the victim of petty national interests, short-sighted political strategies, and ideological conflicts. It was the wish of Dr. Shiotsuki, as it is mine and that of all like-minded people, to leave behind a beautiful earth to our descendants. There can be no doubt that it was also the most earnest desire of those, so eloquently described by Dr. Shiotsuki, who died in suffering at Omura Naval Hospital, of those I saw die around me, and of the brave victims of the atomic bomb who live on.

Dr. Shiotsuki's account of his experience at Omura Naval Hospital first appeared in Japanese in 1978, published by Kobunsha. If his involvement with the atomic bomb and the treatment of its victims had ended with the war, it is doubtful that that slim memoir, no matter how powerful its testimony, would have been published first in his native language and now in English translation. But the fact is, as I have indicated above, that Dr. Shiotsuki continued throughout his life to devote himself to informing the medical world and the larger public about the horrors of the atomic bomb. As more was learned of the true nature of its effects, he had ever more reason to speak out. Nor did resistance to his message in both the medical and the international political community deter him. For that reason, a second part has been added to the present work that gathers together essays and articles written by Dr. Shiotsuki after the war's end. They contain information that supplements his firsthand account and place it in a larger perspective, making Dr. Shiotsuki's personal account a page in the universal testimony to the horror and senselessness of atomic weapons.

Tatsuichiro Akizuki, M.D.
Former Director of St. Francis Hospital
Nagasaki

PREFACE

Thirty-three years ago this summer, I treated atomic bomb victims at Omura Naval Hospital just outside of Nagasaki. I use the word treat, but it was not the type of treatment I can speak of with any pride. The truth is that faced with those appalling injuries and the hitherto unknown effects of radiation disease I was totally baffled and dismayed. All I could really do was see to it that those hovering on the verge of death died as painlessly as possible. In other words, I committed euthanasia; I was a mercy killer.

That experience compels me, as a doctor, to speak out. It torments me with feelings of pain, of contrition, and of regret that no words can ever express. If it were possible, I would like to forget. I would like to keep silent. But circumstances force me to do just the opposite. We are as helpless in the face of atomic weapons today as we were thirty-three years ago. We have made no progress whatsoever; on the contrary, it is my fundamental belief that the situation has gotten increasingly worse.

What progress has medical science made during the past thirty-three years in combating radiation effects? Almost none at all. Even with all the advances of medicine today, it is still impossible to restore a body exposed to radioactivity to normal. The same can be said of the keloid scars caused by the intense heat of the bomb. Although advances in skin-grafting techniques have made it possible to clear up the scarred skin, it is still impossible to cure keloids completely.

Has the production and use of these awesome nuclear weapons been prohibited during the past thirty-three years? As everyone is well aware, the answer is no. On the contrary, the great powers are actually competing to produce weapons a thousand times more powerful than the bombs dropped on Hiroshima and Nagasaki. Occasionally there are discussions about a nuclear disarmament agreement, but these discussions merely serve as bargaining chips in political deals. Even those who engage in these debates do not seriously believe that nuclear weapons will be abolished.

Since Hiroshima and Nagasaki, there have been several photographic exhibits, movies, and literary works dealing with the horrors of the atomic bomb. But what is noticeable about such works is their tendency to indulge in excessive sentimentality or to emphasize only the suffering visible to the naked eye. I do not wish to denigrate emotional appeals but they are, after all, soon forgotten. I believe that only by a cool, scientific understanding of the damage produced by

the atomic bomb can we rid the world of this abom-
inable weapon.

The vast majority of the people in Japan and
throughout the world are now seriously searching for
ways to save humanity from the threat of nuclear
destruction. I am committed to work with them so that
it will never again be necessary to resort to mercy kill-
ing. The writing of this book has been one small effort
in this direction.

Masao Shiotsuki

PART ONE

OMURA NAVAL HOSPITAL

A Flash of Light
and Then the Blast

Thursday, August 9, 1945, 11:02 A.M.

When the atomic bomb fell on Nagasaki, I was stationed nineteen kilometers away from the hypocenter at Omura Naval Hospital. I was twenty-five years old at the time and had been posted to Omura exactly one month earlier, on July 9, as a doctor in training fresh out of Navy Medical School. It was almost as though I had been brought to Omura for the express purpose of encountering the atomic bomb

That day had dawned clear and fair. Billowing clouds trailed through the blue midsummer sky, and the temperature was steadily rising. But a pleasant breeze was raising gentle riplets on the deep blue surface of Omura Bay, bringing relief from the heat to the Naval Hospital on the hill above.

Omura Naval Hospital (or Omura National Hospital, as it is now called) in those days had an inpatient capacity of 2,000 and boasted some of the finest facilities and equipment in the navy. As the war situation deteriorated, however, and the prospect of fighting the decisive stages of the war on the Japanese mainland became ever more imminent, almost all of the less seriously ill were discharged from the hospital to recuperate at home, and the hospital was put into a state of readiness for the expected invasion. The only patients remaining in the wards were critically injured members of the navy's air corps and conscripted factory workers and members of the Women's Volunteer Corps who had sustained injuries during air raids on their factories. To care for these 200 or so patients were 864 doctors, orderlies, nurses, staff members, and military personnel. The hospital was so quiet and uneventful that time hung heavy on our hands.

With a pleasant breeze blowing in from the sea, one could almost doze off and forget that there was a war going on that morning, so peaceful was the hospital. But I was so busy and excited that, far from being able to doze off, I could barely find a moment's peace. For on that day I had been ordered to perform my first important commission as assistant to the officer on duty. The officer on duty exercised absolute control over all the activities within his unit for that day. He also bore total responsibility. As his assistant, all I had to do was rush about forwarding his orders to the lower ranks and conveying information to him from below. It was the first time I had been assigned such duties, however, and I spent most of the morning running the rounds in a considerable state of tension.

But this was not the only important duty I had to

perform that day. Just at that moment the director of the Navy Medical School was on an inspection tour of the hospital, and I had been assigned to perform a "demonstration" (or presentation, in medical-school jargon) on one of the patients for him. I, a mere doctor in training, the lowest in the hierarchy of the navy medical corps, was to explain a patient's condition to the director of the Navy Medical School, a rear admiral! Of course, the director of the hospital (also a rear admiral) and the commissioned officers who formed his entourage would all be there as well.

To make matters worse, the particular patient's case was a difficult one: he was diagnosed as suffering from psychoneurosis of war. In other words, fear experienced on the battlefield had provoked a complicated psychological reaction, which had, in turn, caused actual physical disability. Though this type of illness may at first seem to be a case of malingering, in fact battle wounds sustained by such patients fail to heal in the usual period of time and instead even grow worse. It was of such a difficult case that I, a fledgling doctor with neither sufficient knowledge nor experience, would have to offer an explanation before a group of medical and military dignitaries. I was very excited all morning and would try to snatch time from the demands of assistant to the duty officer to continue my preparations.

The demonstration was scheduled to begin at 11 A.M. The navy prides itself on punctuality, and so on the stroke of eleven I began the very first demonstration of my medical career. What I said or in what order I said it, I have now completely forgotten, but I suppose I had just made some opening remarks when suddenly there was a tremendous flash of light.

I will never forget how bright it was. The windows of the consulting room were wide open, and it was a hot midsummer day. The sky was clear and bright as it often is in Kyushu, especially by the sea, when suddenly an even brighter, more dazzling light flooded in on us. The walls of the hospital room were white and the room was as bright as outdoors. In the midst of all this brightness was a sudden gleam of light like the flash on a camera only longer and far more intense.

I perceived the light as bluish-white, but other people seem to have seen it quite differently. Later when I was able to question some 208 of the survivors of the blast directly, I received diverse replies:

bluish-white	107
bluish-red	54
white	21
greenish-yellow	19
uncertain	7

The strangeness of this light was enough to make anyone afraid, and both the director of the Navy Medical School and the director of the hospital seemed half-paralyzed with fear. Of course, I too was overwhelmed by a sense of apprehension, but at the same time what I had heard about the ''special bomb'' which had been dropped on Hiroshima three days earlier flashed through my mind. I did not know then, however, that this was an atomic bomb. I had only heard from one of the doctors in the air corps that a bomb of unknown nature had been dropped there and that the casualties had been enormous.

"Something is bound to happen next," I thought to myself. The instant the light flashed, I instinctively looked at my wristwatch and stared at the second hand. Ten seconds passed, twenty seconds, thirty seconds . . . nothing happened. Since it would not be proper for me to delay my explanation for too long, I tried to resume my demonstration from where I had left off.

Later on, the Red Cross nurses and enlisted men who were present at the demonstration were to tell me, half in praise and half in jest, "All the rest of us were in a state of tremendous confusion, but you showed splendid composure for someone who was acting as assistant duty officer for the very first time. The only calm persons present when the bomb fell were you and that comatose patient."

Actually, I was far from feeling calm, but I kept telling myself not to panic while on duty, and at the same time I focused all my attention on the movement of the second hand of my watch. A long time seemed to pass. In an abstracted manner, I continued the demonstration, glancing now and then at my wristwatch. Exactly fifty-five seconds after the light had flashed, there was a tremendous boom as though an ordinary bomb of medium size had exploded in the immediate vicinity. The sound was followed by a strong blast and a series of echoes which seemed to explode and resound in every direction. Strangely enough, many of the windows in the back of the hospital shattered though the glass facing the blast remained intact.

Terrified, we all looked at one another. "What was that?" someone said. "Take cover!" another shouted. Being members of the military, there was no panic, but nonetheless admirals and enlisted men alike and almost all the nurses made a dash for the air raid shelter. Almost immediately afterwards, I could hear people—probably the official messengers—running through the hospital shouting, "All hands, take cover. All hands, take cover."

Meanwhile, I was making mental calculations. Fifty-five seconds had elapsed between the flash of light and the boom and blast of the explosion. Since sound travels at 340 meters per second, the bomb had fallen nineteen kilometers away. Consequently, that light must have originated in the sky over Nagasaki.

When I looked around, I realized that the only people left in the room besides myself were the orderly assigned to me and the patient, who was unable to move. I instructed the orderly to take the patient immediately to the air raid shelter, then I rushed down the corridor. The two liaison officers assigned to the duty officer were waiting for me at attention, and together we ran to the command controls. Just then a mass of white cloud was spreading out like a huge umbrella in the clear blue sky over Nagasaki. Its underside harbored a pale pink light, and as it rose higher and higher in the sky, it seemed to increase in size. Underneath the cloud, three white parachutes drifting off to the east were clearly visible to the naked eye.

I immediately grabbed a pair of binoculars and focused in on the parachutes. A long, black cylindrical object was suspended from two of them and a square object was visible on the third. (I later learned that these three objects were radiosondes, instruments for measuring the pressure of the explosion.) The parachutes soon disappeared from our line of vision, but the strange cloud remained. "If only I had my camera with me," I thought and stamped my feet with vexation. When I was a student, I had a German-made Kontax camera, but I was not allowed to take it with me when I entered the service and left it at home. Just as I was regretting not having my camera, an enlisted man came running up with camera in hand. A cameraman was necessary for military purposes even in our unit, and he used the very best camera available at the time.

"Take a picture of that cloud!" I shouted at him. "I already have," he replied. "But I'll take another one." He pushed the shutter. Not long after the picture was taken, about ten minutes after the initial flash of light according to my watch, a light rain began to fall from the clear blue sky. Nothing unusual occurred after that, and about forty minutes later the strange cloud had completely disappeared.

This mysterious event and the sense of uneasiness it produced were the reasons for delaying the all clear signal long after it would normally have been sounded. Everyone except those on duty was taking refuge in the air raid shelter. There was nothing to be done. Restless, I checked the weather conditions:

August 9 (Thursday)

atmospheric conditions	fair
barometric pressure	763.5 mm mercury (in present units, 1,017.7 millibars, high pressure)
temperature	11 A.M. 28°C
humidity	71.0%

These weather conditions were typical for a fine day in August on the west coast of Kyushu. Perhaps recording the weather conditions, like measuring the time elapsed between the flash of light and the bomb blast, reflected my interest in physics, which I had studied quite seriously, though I was by no means an expert.

I soon ran out of things to do and found myself staring blankly from the control room at the sky over Nagasaki. The sky was blue and still, as though no mysterious light or eerie cloud had ever appeared in it. I had a strange sense of foreboding, but at that moment everything seemed so serene. Little did I imagine that beneath that peaceful sky, a terrible disaster, horrifying beyond all comprehension, was unfolding, and that within a very few hours I would be involved in the most heartrending experience of my entire life.

The Doctor-Hater
Who Became a Doctor

I did not enter medical school with the intention of becoming a doctor. But whether I liked it or not, since I had entered the Navy Medical School during wartime, I suddenly found myself confronted at Omura with the victims of the atomic bomb and had to treat those suffering from the effects of atomic radiation. I thus experienced firsthand the horrors that the bomb inflicted.

Ironically, doctors were a breed I had always disliked. My father had graduated from a college on the east coast of the United States and had gone into business there. He had no connection whatsoever with medicine. I was born in the Aoyama district of Tokyo, but my earliest memories are of Seijo, in the western suburbs of Tokyo, where I grew up. At that time the area was still called Kinuta Village. In the middle of the village and through open fields, the roads were laid out in a grid, and cherry saplings were planted on either side. Our house was the seventh to be built in

Seijo. The first was the home of the famous folklorist
Kunio Yanagita. Both houses are still standing today.

Later on when the Odakyu train line extended as far
as Seijo, many intellectuals took up residence there.
The directors and department heads of major hospitals
in Tokyo and several leaders of the medical profession
lived in Seijo. Some doctors opened practices in their
own homes. For some reason, as if by common consent, all these doctors seemed to wear gold-rimmed or
rimless glasses, sport a small moustache, and dangle a
watch on a gold chain over a prominent paunch.

When I was small, I wanted desperately to eat the
delicious-looking sweets that the local farmers' children ate, especially the buns filled with purple bean
paste. Although my parents forbade it, I would whee-
dle enough money from them to buy these forbidden sweets and eat my fill. Very soon, I would get a
stomachache and diarrhea. My parents would worry
and send for the doctor, who soon came bustling in.
All the doctors who came to our house were exactly the
same type, from the glasses and moustache right down
to the pocket watch, be they pediatrician, general prac-
titioner, or the ear and nose specialist who came when
I ran a fever from an inflammation of the inner ear.
Even the way they washed their hands in hot water
from the wash basin my mother or the maid brought
for them was the same. And the inflection in their
voices when they said, "That's a good boy," was identical.

I knew better than anyone else that I was *not* a good
boy. I knew why I was sick, and I could give my own

diagnosis. Child though I was, I felt that no one could talk quite so much nonsense as doctors did.

As I grew up, my antipathy for doctors grew more intense, and I developed a low opinion of them as human beings. Once I contracted conjunctivitis from pollution at a swimming pool and was taken by my mother to an eye specialist, a former professor at the University of Tokyo who was considered the best in Japan. This doctor was extremely polite to my mother and to me, but his attitude towards his nurses and the young woman doctor who was working in his consulting room was shockingly rude and arrogant. I can still remember the violent feeling of anger that welled up inside of me, causing me to forget even the discomfort that my eye was causing.

It may seem strange that I should have chosen to enter medical school at all, but I came to believe that I should study medicine because it was one discipline which could answer scientifically the question, "What is man?" My parents, however, did not want me to go to medical school, and when I was in high school I intended to become an architect. I even submitted an application to the engineering faculty of the University of Tokyo (it was then called Tokyo Imperial University). But when the time came to take the entrance examinations, I changed my mind. Man himself seemed a far more interesting topic of study than the boxes he lived in.

I decided to enter the University of Tokyo School of Medicine and was thinking of spending the following year preparing for the next set of entrance exams without enrolling in school. One of my classmates at Seijo High School happened to be the younger son of Dr. Tokushiro Mitamura, a professor in the University of Tokyo School of Medicine and a leading authority on pathology. When I went to ask his advice, Dr. Mitamura listened to my aspirations then asked me once again whether I *really* wanted to study medicine. I answered, yes, I really did. He thought it over for a while and said, "In that case, go to Sendai. In Sendai you will be able to study real medicine, the kind of medicine you want to study." When such a distinguished authority told me to go to Sendai (the city in northeastern Japan that was the site of Tohoku Imperial University) instead of saying, "Come to Tokyo where I teach," I was inclined to believe him.

And so I went to Sendai, half for pleasure and half to tour the facilities there. I did not know much about the workings of the school, but the city as seen from Mount Aoba was very peaceful and appealing to me. My mind was made up. Fortunately I passed the entrance examinations on my first try, and I became a student at the Tohoku Imperial University Faculty of Medicine.

Once I had entered the university, I understood why Dr. Mitamura had told me to go there. Among the many distinguished members of the medical world who were on the faculty was Professor Toshio Kurokawa, who later became honorary director of the Cancer Research Hospital. Studying directly under men of such high personal standards and wide knowledge, I learned that medicine was first and foremost a humanitarian calling, an academic discipline for the betterment of the human race. Freedom of thought also flourished in Sendai. The school resisted pressure from the military and refused to allow military training of its students right up until the very end.

Student life there was physically comfortable as well. When I returned to Tokyo during vacations, at the sushi shops I was surprised to find a piece of some totally unfamiliar fish resting on top of rice mixed with buckwheat and seaweed. In Sendai, however, there was plenty of white rice, and fresh fish and shellfish were brought in from Matsushima, Shiogama, Kamaishi, and elsewhere. Draft beer from the large breweries was available everywhere throughout the city.

It was in this sort of atmosphere that I engaged in the study of medicine. But soon graduation came pressing in on me, or rather, in compliance with the demands of the military, the course of study was shortened. Students in other faculties had been sent off to the battlefield in a general mobilization of students, and every able-bodied man among civilians as well was called into the army. As a consequence, both the army and navy were able to fill their battle quotas, but there was an acute shortage of military doctors. There were not that many medical schools in those days, and the number of graduates each year was, by present standards, unbelievably small. Special medical schools to train doctors rapidly had been set up throughout Japan, but even these could not fill the needs right away.

And so the military contrived to speed up the course

of study in all the medical schools. Since, in any event, we would be taken into one of the services once we graduated, it did not matter what we studied; there was no point in learning any more than would be of direct use to a military doctor. As a last-ditch measure, the summer vacation before our final year of school was given over to practical training—what would now be called an internship.

To take advantage of the students' return to their home towns, hospitals near home were designated as the sites of their internships. Because my home was in Tokyo and thanks to the recommendations of my professors, I did my training at St. Luke's Hospital in Tsukiji, which had incorporated the most advanced foreign methods of medical treatment available in those days. All that remained was for me to wait for graduation the following year, then join either the army or the navy. That choice was left up to the individual. I did not particularly care one way or the other, but a greater number of my relatives had some involvement with the navy.

To take the story back a few years, one of my relatives had been chief gunner on the cruiser *Atago,* and he had shown me around the ship when I was a little boy. Captain Koga, who later became commander in chief of the combined fleet, was ship's captain. To board a warship was the fondest dream of every boy in those days. Perhaps it was a special feeling of affinity engendered then that led me to take the entrance exams for the Naval Academy when I was in middle school.

The Naval Academy and the Army Officers' School were the twin pillars of the elite course. Naturally their entrance examinations were extremely difficult. For that very reason, they were worth the challenge, and I took them not because I wanted to become a naval officer but as a kind of practice examination. Perhaps not taking them seriously worked in my favor, for I passed them easily. I was quite surprised, but my mother was even more so. I suppose she felt that even if she would one day have to sacrifice her son for her country, handing him over to the military while he was still in middle school was a bit too soon. She appealed indirectly to the head military doctor of the academy, who failed me in the physical examination, though I was perfectly healthy.

What would have become of me if things had taken their natural course then and I had entered the navy? Probably I would have died at sea somewhere. Even if I had been lucky enough to survive, Dr. Shiotsuki, the medical student, would never have come into existence. At any rate, due to circumstances in my childhood, I chose the navy instead of the army.

Graduation was speeded up and set for September 1945. Here, too, fate intervened. If my graduation had been as originally scheduled, I would still have been a student when the war ended. But instead something totally unexpected happened: the military, because of its pressing need for doctors, speeded up the process still further and put graduation six months ahead of schedule. For that reason we were provisionally graduated in March 1945 and forced out of medical school.

Forthwith I became a student at the Navy Medical School and received special military training for a period lasting three months. Then I received orders to serve at Omura Naval Hospital in Nagasaki Prefecture, and on July 6 my companions and I boarded a reserved train to take us to our new assignment.

Trains in those days were slow to begin with, and they were further delayed by air raids. The train would go a certain distance, then there would be an air raid alert and it would stop. The all clear would sound and the train would start up again. This process was repeated throughout the day and into the night, and it took four days to get to Nagasaki. It was indeed a long journey to my fated rendezvous with the atomic bomb.

I should explain here something about my status as a doctor in training. As I mentioned earlier, those of us who were scheduled to graduate in September 1945 had had our course of study cut short by six months and were provisionally graduated in March. The faculty association of the imperial universities, however, did not let the military have its way entirely. In the face of the real shortage of military doctors, the faculty agreed to the military's demands within certain precise limits, but they adamantly refused to step beyond those limits and make a mockery of the educational process. They allowed us to graduate in March, but in a last show of defiance refused to give us our diplomas until the prescribed date in September. Perhaps we might call their decision an attempt to preserve their self-respect. But in order to preserve their self-respect, we graduates found ourselves on the receiving end of a considerable backlash from the military.

In the normal course of events, a graduate of a university faculty of medicine was commissioned a lieutenant junior grade upon entering the navy, while a graduate of a specialized medical school was commissioned an ensign. The military, however, was sorely perplexed about what rank to give those of us who had graduated but had no graduation diplomas. And so, with the condition that we would automatically become lieutenants in September, we were given the lowest possible rank of ''doctor in training,'' a rank unprecedented in the annals of naval history.

But though our status as doctors in training made us somewhat like outsiders, our actual hospital duties as members of a unit in active front-line service were horrendous. In the vicinity there were several naval air bases and war-supply factories, which almost every day were exposed to air raids. After every raid, soldiers, factory workers, and members of the Women's Volunteer Corps were carried to the hospital, their legs and arms blown off.

The first assignments for us doctors in training were to assist at these ghastly operations. We did not then have the advanced methods of anesthesia that we have now, and surgery was extremely brutal. I can never forget even now the sight of those young people who let out piercing screams as the scalpel began to probe, and then breathed their last. I am embarrassed to admit that there were times when I fainted, bathed in blood in the midst of that hell.

But those experiences proved invaluable, for without them I could never have been able one month later to deal with one victim after another in an even greater hell, spawned by the atomic bomb.

First Reports from the Inferno

By the time everything had returned to normal at Omura, the sun was rising higher and higher in the sky. The minutes ticked away in eerie silence. There was nothing for me to do, and I stared absently at the sky over Nagasaki. In a little while the first report came in over the military communications network: "Special bomb dropped on Nagasaki. Scores of casualties, city in flames. Bomb probably same type as fell on Hiroshima."

The duty officer, who conveyed this information to me, added, "Something terrible seems to have happened. I am going to report the news to the head of the hospital. Wait for me here." Then he rushed off. I slumped down into the chair in the deserted officers' room. Normally I would be spending this time in my own room resting after lunch. To the weight of the pressures I had been under since morning had been added one unexpected and totally incomprehensible event after another, and physically and mentally I was completely exhausted. Perhaps that was the reason that I dozed off while waiting for my superior, who was a long time in returning. I have no idea how long I slept.

I was suddenly awakened by what seemed a loud voice, though my superior was not actually shouting at me. The officer on duty was Dr. Jinnai, a lieutenant junior grade and an extremely able person whom I respected very much. He told me that he had been ordered to form and head the Omura Naval Hospital Special Relief Mission and go immediately to the scene of the bombing. While he was away, he said, I was to act as duty officer in his place.

This was an unexpected development. I, a mere doctor in training, the lowest of all naval officers, found myself in the position of having to assume the responsibilities of the duty officer and to take command and make prompt decisions on all matters from then on.

After he had rapidly run through the matters that needed to be attended to, he asked as a kind of afterthought, looking as though he wanted to bite me, "As assistant to the officer on duty, why didn't you immediately order everyone to take cover when the bomb fell?" I was at a loss for an answer. "No need to reply now. You can explain later," he said and rushed off.

Today, more than thirty years later, that question remains unanswered. Why did he ask me, since I had absolutely no authority to give such an order? Probably he was confused. But the very fact that such a fine model of a military man could be thrown into this state

of consternation shows how unusual were the events of
that day.

The air raid alert was lifted not long afterward, and
the relief mission led by Lieutenant Jinnai loaded
drugs and medical supplies onto a navy bus and drove
out the hospital gates. About five o'clock that evening,
a telephone call came in from the mayor of Omura asking the head of the naval hospital for his assistance in
treating bomb casualties. The number of dead and
wounded in Nagasaki was beyond calculation. Nagasaki Medical College and all the treatment centers
both within the city and on its periphery had been demolished.

The mayor was asking us at Omura Naval Hospital
to accept at least a thousand casualties. They would be
put on board a specially prepared train at Urakami,
then carried by trucks and other available transport
from Omura Station to the hospital. The first train was
scheduled to arrive at eight or nine that evening. The
mayor thanked us for our cooperation and then rang
off.

As acting duty officer, I immediately ordered that
the wards and operating rooms be readied and instructed the staff to fortify themselves by eating dinner
as soon as possible. I myself had no time for dinner
and had forgotten to eat lunch that day as well. Later
on I felt very hungry, but my empty stomach may
have been a blessing in disguise.

Just before eight o'clock, word came from Omura
Station that a large number of casualties had just arrived there by train and were now on their way to the

hospital by truck and military transport. Straightaway I went and stood at the entrance to the hospital. It would be my responsibility as acting duty officer to direct the admission of the wounded. All the stretchers that we had were piled up high as a mountain in the entrance hall, and many noncommissioned officers, soldiers, and nurses were standing in readiness there.

As a precaution against air attack, the restrictions on lighting were more stringent than usual that evening. The experience of the special bombing earlier that day had made us especially rigorous about putting the blackout into effect. All personnel held flashlights in their hands, but were careful not to switch them on unnecessarily.

Finally automobile horns sounded in the darkness and the truck and military transports arrived. The military transports were filled to capacity with patients, but the truck was even worse. In the open loading compartment, people had been stacked until there was no space left, and the living were indistinguishable from the dead. The sight was so horrifying that unthinkingly I cried out in dismay.

Their hair had been singed by the fire, their clothes were in rags, and their exposed flesh was burned and covered in blood. When we shone our flashlights on them, we could see countless fragments of glass, wood, and metal still embedded in their faces and backs and arms and legs. It was hard to believe that these were human beings. To make matters worse, a pitch-black substance like coal tar adhered to the faces and backs of all of them without exception. One look at this sight and I said to myself, "The war is over. If butchery as horrible as this were to continue, people would all choose to commit suicide."

The shock the NCOs and ordinary soldiers had received was undoubtedly just as great as my own. Perhaps it was presumptuous of me, but I had thought that it was my job as duty officer to give orders and that the actual admission of the wounded into the hospital was the NCOs' and soldiers' responsibility. But they all stood there looking on and holding their breath; not one of them moved. Many of those NCOs were combat veterans, and some of them had many years of combat experience. Some had made their way through a hail of bullets as members of naval brigades or had saved themselves by crawling out of sinking warships. But even men with such long service behind them flinched at this sight and would not budge.

I realized that I had to rouse myself and fulfil my obligations for the absent duty officer. This sense of responsibility stirred me to action. An experienced officer could probably have let out a roar and gotten the NCOs and soldiers to move. But since I lacked the necessary self-confidence to give orders, I immediately jumped into the open loading area of the truck. An awful stench assaulted my nostrils. The smell of death was mixed with the distinctive odor, somewhat like roast cuttlefish, of burned flesh. Under ordinary circumstances, I would have vomited. It turned out to be fortunate that I had not had the time to eat either lunch or dinner and my stomach was empty.

I lifted up one person from the pile of bodies. Several NCOs came rushing over to the truck, turned on their flashlights and waited in readiness below. The first person had been burned so badly it was impossible to tell in the light of the flashlights whether it was a man or a woman. My hands grew quite slippery from the oozing burns and the sticky tarlike substance, but somehow or other I was able to lower the first patient down to the NCOs' waiting hands.

The next victim was covered with blisters which had swollen so much it was hard to believe that this was a human being. It was a man, but I have no idea how old he might have been. When I had finished passing him on to the NCOs, I let out another gasp, for beneath him had been a dead baby. Probably it had been crushed to death under the stacks of wounded bodies, jostled by the movement of the truck over the winding mountain road on the way to the hospital. The baby was already cold. I had no time to use my stethoscope, so I put my ear to its chest. The heart had stopped beating. Was its mother somewhere on the truck? I wondered. Or was she too already dead? Probably the baby had been piled in with the others indiscriminately and, separated from its mother's protecting arms, had fallen under some dying victim with the movement of the truck and had been crushed to death. A feeling of pity wrung my heart, but I had no time to give way to sentiment. It was more important to get the living off the truck as soon as possible and give them medical attention.

Soon the NCOs jumped on the truck and began helping me hand down the wounded. The tempo of relief

operations quickened to the pace of activity on a battlefield. It was my responsibility to direct this activity,
and so I left the job of unloading the wounded to the
soldiers and, with the senior doctors, applied myself to
diagnosing their injuries. Burn victims were taken to
the wards on the first floor. The wounded were carried
to the operating rooms. Many were already dead on
arrival. They had probably survived the train ride to
Omura, but had died while being carried by truck over
the mountain road. Their bodies were taken to the
mortuary.

With no time for us to rest, the second and third
loads of patients arrived. Stopping only to unload, all
the trucks turned around and headed back to pick up
the next group of patients waiting at Omura Station.
The distance between the station and the hospital was
about four kilometers, and I do not know how many
times the trucks shuttled back and forth. One truck
would pull up and unload dozens of people at the entrance to the hospital. Before these had been divided
up and taken to wards, surgery, or the mortuary, the
next truck would arrive, and without letup the process
was repeated.

Meanwhile experienced doctors, nurses, and orderlies were administering first aid and operating on the
injured. As officer on duty, I remained stationed at the
hospital entrance to receive patients. The chaos and
confusion and the gruesome spectacle presented there
was a vision of hell. "You looked just like some kind
of demon yourself that night, Dr. Shiotsuki," one of
the orderlies told me when we were talking about our

impressions of that evening some time later. It is not difficult to imagine what gave him that impression. I had had no time to use my stethoscope and my face from my cheeks to my mouth was covered with blood from where I had laid my ears directly on the victims' chests to listen for their heartbeats and ascertain whether they were alive or dead. Only my eyes glittered in the darkness, and I may indeed have looked like one of the man-eating demons of hell.

Naturally the critically wounded had been brought here as quickly as possible, in the hope of saving their lives. The injuries of those on the trucks that came later were less serious, and the victims in the last truckloads were well enough to get off the trucks by themselves. Even so, none of these people was wearing shoes. They were barefoot and their feet were covered with mud. The clothes of men and women alike had been torn to pieces and were nothing but rags. Something like a piece of cloth dangled from the back of one man who was naked from the waist up. Looked at more closely, it proved to be a strip of skin which had peeled off leaving the subcutaneous tissue exposed and raw, something we often encounter when performing dissections. Since this type of injury was considered mild enough for the patient to be sent with the later groups, the horrible condition of the casualties in the first groups brought in to us can be inferred. They were barely alive, their breathing faint, their bodies burned black, with not enough strength even to complain of their misery.

According to hospital records, 758 people were

admitted that evening. We started accepting them around eight o'clock and finished, for the time being, at eleven. For so many recently wounded to be admitted to one hospital in the space of three hours is undoubtedly unprecedented. And this was only a small fraction of the victims of this single bomb blast.

Midnight. The time for the changeover of duty officers had arrived, and I was relieved of my twenty-four-hour shift as assistant to the officer of the day. Lieutenant Jinnai, who had been duty officer that day, was still away on the relief mission to Nagasaki, but I was relieved from my duties on his behalf. Though this duty shift was over, I had no time to rest. I immediately had to take charge of the medical treatment of patients assigned to my care in Ward 8. But there was no treatment, really, that we could give them. People who had arms and legs blown off, bones broken, glass and wood fragments embedded in them, were taken to surgery, where experienced surgeons operated on them one after another. Most of the other patients were treated for burns.

Almost all the patients suffered from burns. Medically speaking there are four degrees of burns: in first degree burns (combustio erythematosa), the skin only turns red; in second degree burns (combustio bullosa), blisters form on and around the flushed area; in third degree burns (combustio escharotica), the tissue is destroyed; and in fourth degree burns (combustio carbonisata), an extreme form of third degree burn, the body is carbonized to a black color. Most of our patients suffered from second or third degree burns.

If the second degree burn is limited to a small area, it can be appropriately treated by applying ointment to the burn and giving the patient injections of glucose and vitamin compounds. But if second and third degree burns cover an extensive area of the body, nothing can be done except wait for the patient to die. The burns on all of my patients were so horrible they surpassed the limits of medical knowledge.

After each patient had been treated, he was carried into a hospital room. Most of the patients, however, still lay on sheets spread on the floor in the hall, groaning in pain. Blackout curtains covered the windows, and the hospital was like a steambath, making the distinctive smell of burned flesh and the stench of death all the stronger. In the midst of this heat and stench lay people who had no chance of surviving, for whom nothing remained but agony.

"My god, what am I to do?" I thought to myself. Confronted with a reality in which nothing I had learned from medical textbooks was of the slightest avail, all I could do was grit my teeth and try in some way to relieve their pain. To patients crying for water, I brought water and let them drink their fill. For many this was the last drink. It is common knowledge that patients who can respond to treatment should not be allowed to drink water, because they might suffocate or go into shock. But how could I refuse water to these people who wanted it so desperately, knowing as I did that they were going to die?

The same feelings led me to give morphine to patients whose suffering was unbearable, so that they could forget their agony even for just a little while. I also gave the nurses and orderlies permission to administer morphine without waiting for a doctor's orders.

As a result, I assisted in committing euthanasia. Or to put it another way, I was a mercy killer. Those people died peacefully, I believe, their pain and agony relieved. But even today I myself feel terrible pain and agony that as a doctor I could not help them to live but could only send one after another of them to a painless death. My own torment will continue until the moment I too lose consciousness in death.

At the Center of the Bomb—
An Eyewitness Account

And so the night of August 9 came to an end. Of the 758 patients admitted, nearly 100 died that first night. By about 5:30 in the morning the first stage of on-the-spot emergency treatment for each patient was over. The short summer night had ended and outside it was already light. The blackout curtains in the hospital wards were pulled aside.

Seen again in the light of day, the bomb victims were far more grotesque than the flashlights and faint electric lights of the previous night had made them seem, so horrible in fact that one instinctively averted one's eyes from them. Our patients' suffering and death did not abate for one moment nor could their medical treatment and nursing be interrupted to allow us sleep or rest.

Why did so many people have to endure so much agony? In order to answer this question, it is necessary to discuss the frightening operation of the atomic bomb. The special characteristic of the atomic bomb is that it produces simultaneously an explosive force, high heat, and radiation, all incalculably more powerful than anything previously known. By expert estimate, the area of one square meter directly under the point of explosion (the bomb dropped on Nagasaki exploded about five hundred meters above the ground) received five to ten tons of pressure from the blast—a force equivalent to that of a large dump truck loaded with gravel striking a pedestrian at top speed.

As a result, immediate contact with the blast was enough to tear a person limb from limb and make his eyes and organs burst out of his body. In addition, a great number of the victims died as a result of wounds indirectly caused by the bomb, received when buildings collapsed on them or from fragments propelled by the blast. In fact, the force of the blast and its strange effects are almost impossible for someone who has never seen its victims to imagine—for example, glass fragments were propelled violently into the entire surface of patients' arms and legs and backs. If you visualize the fragments of beer bottles sometimes embedded in concrete on the tops of walls to act as a deterrent to thieves you will have some idea of what these people looked like, only there were dozens of these fragments, hundreds of them, all over their bodies. Some of these fragments of glass and iron had pierced to the bone, embedded themselves deeply into the arm and leg muscles, and penetrated even to the lungs and stomach.

Another example of the force of the explosion can be seen in the case of a young farmer who was working in a field about two kilometers from the center of the blast. He was thrown to the ground by the explosion, and though he fell on soft, freshly tilled earth, his thigh bone broke right in two. In an ordinary explosion, no broken bones or other external injuries could possibly occur from contact with soft, tilled earth, no matter how hard the victim was thrown to the ground. Yet another victim's skull was pierced by a small branch from a tree, still pliant from its midsummer growth. Though an ordinary explosion might cause a branch to break off a tree, it could not conceivably turn it into a weapon that would pierce the hard bone structure of the skull.

The next cause of injuries was the heat of the blast. At the moment of explosion, this heat is said to be equivalent to the heat of the sun if it were to descend to a point several hundred meters above our heads. Near the center of the atomic bomb blast, paper piled solidly up to the ceiling of a warehouse was reduced to ashes in an instant. In a conventional fire, books usually burn on the outside while the insides remain uncharred. Nevertheless, most of the paper piled ceiling high turned completely to ash even in the center of the stack. From this fact, one can easily imagine how intense the heat must have been.

This intense heat came into direct contact with human bodies. Under normal conditions, it is said, cremation is not so easily accomplished; considerable heat and technical skill are required to burn a corpse completely. Many people were thrown into the atomic bomb's fiery furnace while still alive and were totally reduced to ashes. Even people at some distance from the hypocenter were critically burned by direct exposure to this heat, and in many instances their burns proved fatal. A survey of patients admitted to Omura Naval Hospital showed that 97 percent of the burns sustained were caused by heat from the explosion and a mere 3 percent could be attributed to the fires that spread afterward.

In addition to the force of the explosion and the heat it produced, the frightening effects of radiation began to reveal their merciless nature to us about one or two days after the bomb had fallen. I will describe them in the sequence they followed and write about them in more detail later rather than discuss them here.

What was the situation like in the devastated area immediately after the bomb fell? A person I knew very well gave me an eyewitness account of the scene. Yasumasa Iyonaga was then serving as chief orderly at Omura Naval Hospital. He was an enlisted man from Fukuoka Prefecture and had entered the navy by a route completely different from mine. He, too, was twenty-five years old. When I first arrived at Omura, the sight of him devotedly and selflessly attending to patients' needs engraved itself indelibly on my heart. Although he had many more years of experience than I, my status as officer placed me above him. In spite of this official barrier, a personal friendship blossomed which was able to bridge the gap. Today Iyonaga is involved in the youth movement in Fukuoka, and our friendship still flourishes. On that day in August, he was a member of the Omura Naval Hospital Special

Relief Mission led by Lieutenant Jinnai, which rushed to Nagasaki right after the bombing. He later told me what he had witnessed there.

CHIEF ORDERLY IYONAGA'S STORY

"As the relief squad bus drew closer and closer to Nagasaki, an indescribably horrible spectacle began to unfold before our eyes. The trees that remained were only bare branches; though it was midsummer, the landscape looked like a mountainside in winter. Those buildings still standing had all tumbled over to one side, but as we approached the center of the explosion, they had been pressed down from above and crushed completely out of shape. Reinforced concrete buildings had collapsed as though they were paper boxes. Everywhere one looked were bare trees, piles of debris, and splinters of wood—the landscape of hell. The area had met with a truly formidable bombardment, that was obvious.

"I do not know how many dead bodies we saw along the way. Most of them were charred black, almost carbonized. We repeatedly encountered long lines of people fleeing the city. Their clothes were in rags and had turned completely black as though painted with coal tar, and their hair had burned off so it was difficult to tell the men from the women. I do not know whether they were searching for aid stations or looking for water, but they all plodded wearily forward. They did not hold their arms by their sides but let them dangle in front of them, like ghosts.

"None of them said a word. We had treated many air raid victims before, but the circumstances here were totally different from anything we had previously encountered. Ordinarily a wounded man will clench his teeth but finally cry out if he is in pain. He will call out for help and yell at you if you do not give him the proper treatment. But these people did not say a single word or utter a single cry. Every one of them tottered by in total silence. There is no other way to describe them but as a procession of the living dead.

"Several people had fallen and were unable to move. You would think that they were already dead, but then you would see their eyes flicker as though they were watching our bus pass by. If I had not been a member of the relief squad acting under orders, I would probably have jumped off the bus and tried to take care of them. I think Lieutenant Jinnai felt the same way. But as a relief squad, we first had to receive our orders from Nagasaki General Headquarters, and so our bus raced in that direction.

"When we arrived, we were made to wait in the basement air raid shelter. I was very restless and anxious to get to work, but as I glanced around the empty room I noticed a propaganda leaflet lying on a desk. It was well printed, quite different from the cheap mimeographed leaflets one often saw. A drawing depicted the United States and the Soviet Union shaking hands. Beneath it was written in Japanese: 'We have perfected the atomic bomb. End the war, Japan.'

"Even we soldiers had heard vague rumors about the atomic bomb, to the effect that it was something the size of a matchbox that possessed tremendous destructive power. But it had not occurred to me that the destruction I had just seen was the result of the atomic bomb, and even if someone had told me, I do not think I would have had any real sense of the connection between the two.

"Just then a military police officer came rushing in. He grabbed the leaflet from the table and with an extremely threatening attitude demanded whether any of us had read it. I realized that the leaflet contained highly classified information and pretended that I had not even noticed it. If I had inadvertently mentioned that I had read it, I suspect I would have been in serious trouble. The MP snatched up the leaflet and left the room.

"Our unit was divided into two groups, and we commenced our relief activities. The first group, under the direct command of Lieutenant Jinnai, headed toward Urakami. I was next in seniority and was put in charge of the second group, which headed to the first aid station at Inasa Elementary School. By now it was completely dark. I had the bus stop in front of the Inasa police station and went inside to establish contact with relief operations. It was pitch black inside the police station and deathly still. The building was partly destroyed, but someone should have been there. 'Is anyone there?' I called, but no one answered. It was as silent as a tomb. 'That's strange,' I thought and shone my flashlight around. Involuntarily I let out a gasp and stopped in my tracks.

"On the rubble-littered floor lay so many casualties

you could scarcely move without stepping on them. In the darkness I had thought the place was totally deserted, but instead dozens, no, hundreds of people were lying there quietly, unable to make a single sound. It was surreal. The sight of these people was far more grotesque even than the procession of survivors I had caught sight of in the burned-out ruins of the city. Which of these people were still living, which had already died?—even these questions were difficult to answer. Just then some of the victims noticed the light of my flashlight and in faint voices began to ask for water. The voices were so low and so agonized that they seemed to come from the depths of the earth. We immediately set about giving first aid, and all of us worked continuously for more than twenty hours, without a moment's rest, until we ran out of medical supplies and had to return to Omura.

"Once we arrived at the hospital, we were assigned to ward duty, without being given a chance to rest. The hospital wards were filled to overflowing with wounded just like those we had seen in Nagasaki. The victims died one after another, and we could do nothing but look on helplessly. I remember gathering together the orderlies and nurses who worked under me and saying, 'Up until now it has been our duty to give aid and comfort to the sick. But most of these people are well advanced on the road to death, and we cannot save them. Their medical treatment is no longer our main concern. Rather than increase their sufferings with treatment that will ultimately do them no good, try to make their deaths as easy and painless as

possible. If you have any religious convictions, now is
the time for you to show them and give moral support
to the dying. Look after each and every one of them as
tenderly as possible and stay with them until the end
comes.' And then I behaved in a way unbecoming a
soldier and in spite of myself burst into tears.''

"The MP Cried"—
Testimony of a Bomb Victim

To follow Iyonaga's account, I would like to introduce the testimony of an actual victim of the bomb, whom I will refer to as Mr. T. N. Mr. N. received contusions on his hips and both legs when the ceiling fell on him at a factory near the hypocenter. He was admitted to Omura Naval Hospital and was one of the patients in my ward. He is now a teacher of English. There are numerous eyewitness accounts of the atomic bomb, but these excerpts from Mr. N.'s diary seem to me to be among the most vivid and immediately felt. I have collected them together in the form of a letter to me.

"Dear Dr. Shiotsuki:

"It is almost thirty-three years now since we met. Though we had not known each other before, you became someone I will never forget for the rest of my life, all because of the terrible way the war was brought to an end. The workings of divine providence are strange indeed.

"As I am sure you remember, Nagasaki was so vital and alive that morning under a clear blue sky and bright sun that you could almost forget there was a war going on. At that time, I was a technical trainee at a munitions plant belonging to M— Manufacturing, and as an apprentice technician was busily engaged in both specialized studies and on-the-job training. On August 9, I was attending morning classes with forty-three classmates. Food rationing was strict, and that morning we had eaten only rice gruel mixed with dried greens. By now we were overcome with hunger pangs and, from the sound of it, some of the senior students in the back of the class had already begun to open their lunch boxes.

"I looked at my watch. It was five minutes to eleven. Lunchtime was at 11:50. Try to hold out just a little longer, I thought, and made my eyes skim the manual on torpedoes we were studying. Just then an indescribable wind blew by and the pile of lumber stacked in the nearby yard rattled. It was my first experience of this kind, and I did not fully understand what was happening, but I instinctively realized that it was a bomb. Right away, I lay down on my right side between the rows of desks. My left leg was not quick enough, though, and the knee got wedged between the desk and chair. This was the awkward position I was in when the ceiling and ridge of the roof collapsed on top of us. My mind at that moment raced to thoughts of death, and I remembered my parents and brothers and younger sister, who I thought I would never see again.

"A long time seemed to pass, though perhaps it was not so very long after all. A heat such as I had never experienced before—so oppressive and sultry I thought I would vomit—overwhelmed me. But for some strange reason my surroundings seemed locked in silence. I kept thinking that something would happen, but nothing did.

"I could not hear the noises that just a moment before had resounded so briskly through the factory, nor the sound of trains running on the Nagasaki main line nearby, nor even human voices. My ears echoed with the sense of stillness one often hears on a snowy winter evening. It was the stillness of death.

"Now I became aware of my own plight. Under ordinary circumstances I would have been crushed to death, but fortunately I had fallen in the empty space between two desks, an area about one meter wide, and the ceiling and roof had buckled and fallen over the desks. For the moment my life had been spared. 'Are you all right?' 'Get out of there quickly.' Suddenly the sound of voices broke the silence. They belonged to my classmates who had been at the back of the classroom eating an early lunch. I later learned that the blast had thrown several of them out of the window. They had landed on the incline of a ditch which formed the boundary between us and the normal school next door—with their lunch boxes in one hand and their chopsticks in the other. Strangely enough they were completely unhurt.

"When the shock passed and they returned to their senses, they immediately began to call out to those of us who had been trapped under the falling building. 'Get out of there quickly.' 'The fire is spreading.' Urged on by their cries, someone was trying to crawl out from the debris. I could hear him, but I myself could not move. My friend next to me was also pinned down. 'We're here, over here!' we yelled as loud as we could. Everyone pitched in and helped, and fortunately my friend and I were pulled out just before the flames reached us. As I crawled out of the rubble, I was stunned by what I saw.

"Everything seem covered with some kind of mist. The air was yellow and oppressive. The steel skeleton of the factory, which had towered over us only minutes before, undulated like melted jelly, and the interior was in flames. Our classroom had been crushed like a matchbox. From that point on, I began to lose consciousness. My critically injured friend and I were put on top of doors and carried toward the station by our uninjured friends.

"On the way there, I remember hearing calls for help from groaning voices that seemed to come from underground. My friends were taking us to a first aid center, but they could not let these voices from beneath the earth go unanswered. They set us down and started digging. 'Isn't there anything to dig with?' they asked. 'Use these splinters of wood or anything else you can find, but dig! Quickly!' The voices sounded frantic. The surrounding area was becoming a sea of flames. I again lost consciousness from pain and shock and have no recollection of whether those trapped people were rescued or not.

"When I regained awareness, I had been carried to Nagasaki Station. I realized that from here I was to be taken somewhere and that we were waiting for crews to restore the train lines to service. We had to wait a long, long time. My pain was so intense and so excruciating that I thought I would die. I would lose consciousness and then revive. This happened over and over again. Finally I was carried on board the train. Whether from a sense of relief or from a lessening of the shock and pain, from then on I became a bit more lucid and was able to take in what was going on around me.

"The inside of the train was a box crammed full of charred and festering ghosts. People wearing something that covered their bodies were so few you could count them. Most were in rags and some were practically naked. The smell of burned flesh mixed with the sultry air. The agony I felt from the nausea and headache that the smell caused was almost unbearable. Gasping for breath, we finally arrived at Isahaya Station. Many were carried off the train there to be taken at once to treatment centers. We waited at the station a long time. Those who could move crawled to the platform to escape the stench. The broiling sun finally sank in the west and night fell, but the humidity only increased in intensity.

"I saw two seriously injured boys who looked like brothers. 'I can't make it any further,' the younger said. 'You go to the hospital by yourself. Give my love to Mother.' 'Don't be a fool,' the other answered. 'What are you talking about? I can't last much longer either, but let's keep going.' Both the younger brother who had given up and the older brother who was urging him on spoke in weak, exhausted voices. I will never forget the sight of them standing on tottering legs helping one another with the last desperate shreds of strength left to them. After they had disappeared, a pool of blood glowed black in the darkness in the place where they had sat.

"On that midsummer day, we had nothing to eat or to drink and could barely contain our suffering under those blazing skies. What we wanted more than anything else was a drink of water. Those with scorched and festering skin must have wanted it even more than the rest of us, I expect. Every time the train stopped, with the last strength left to them the people on board would ask the MP on duty on the platform to bring them some water. 'You fools,' one MP said brutally to them, 'Don't you know that if you drink water, that will be the end of you?' 'We don't care. Give us water.' These mortally wounded people leaned out the windows and stretched out their hands to the MP. 'Please, please give us water.' The MP was probably under strict orders not to give us water under any circumstances, and there was nothing he could do except turn away.

"Our train remained at that station for a long time. Presently the MP pressed a white-gloved hand to his eyes. An MP, as terrifying as the devil himself to soldiers and civilians alike, was crying. In the gathering darkness of the station, the white of a glove shone against his face; in the deepening stillness of this day of hell, it spoke eloquently.

"We arrived at Omura Station. I do not remember how many trucks left before I was finally loaded onto one, but it seems to me that I had to wait quite a long time. I do remember being loaded onto the back of a truck at the instruction of an MP and I remember, too, the almost hopeless feeling I had as I was carried in it over that dark mountain road. Nor will I ever forget the joy I felt when we pulled up at the entrance to Omura Naval Hospital and were met by people in white. I really felt that I had met my saviors in hell.

"We were carried to a large room on the first floor and there we heard, as if in a dream, a voice asking if any of us wanted water. Water was then poured out from a large tea kettle for us. How delicious it tasted! There are no words to describe it. I was given emergency treatment and then taken to a private room on the second floor. The soldiers and nurses were very kind to me and I was put to bed, but I could hear the groans and screams of people receiving treatment on the floor beneath me and was unable to sleep.

"There were people far more critically injured than I who were gasping in pain and corpses so grotesque I could not bear to look at them. Why did this have to happen? What will become of the war? What will become of Japan? As I was turning these thoughts over in my despondent heart, I finally reached the limits of exhaustion. I forgot the pain in my legs and fell sound asleep."

Hallucinations of Whiteness

The morning of August 10 dawned. While we were pondering once again the grotesque sight of the injured as they were now revealed to us by the light of day, a steady stream of new patients was being sent in to us. Had they spent the night groaning in pain in the darkness with no one to lend them a helping hand? The number of patients and the terrible nature of their wounds were almost exactly the same as those admitted the previous night. In fact, by having been left untended throughout the night, their symptoms had rapidly advanced, as had their suffering.

About seventy of these patients were admitted to my ward, and the chaos of the previous night's scene of carnage repeated itself. I must point out that when I use the words chaos and carnage I am speaking from the vantage point of those of us who were administering treatment and tending wounds, not from the patients' perspective. What had been true the night before held true as well that morning—not one of the patients cried out or gave any signs of the hellish agony they were in. It was odd, in fact, that almost no one complained of pain even though they had sustained the most hideous injuries. How eerily frightening was the way they went to their deaths in silent suffering.

Years later I investigated whether there were any accounts of the psychology of people in the midst of some enormous disaster. I never found any satisfactory information on the subject, but I did discover accounts of the same phenomenon of dazed passivity in less serious cases, such as the victims of major earthquakes or of floods caused by typhoons, or soldiers pushed to the ultimate extremity on the battlefield. I knew that some European doctors referred to this phenomenon as "the disaster syndrome." The silent suffering of the atomic bomb victims must be this syndrome's most extreme example. Or was it something altogether different in nature? This I can say: those people never lost the awareness of their physical or psychological suffering. On the contrary, they were completely lucid and their reactions were normal. Nevertheless, they locked their suffering up in silence and in stillness. This was one mystery I felt that I had to solve in order to better understand my fellow man.

When the patients were brought in to us the second day, the problem confronting us was exactly the same as on that first night—what treatment should we give them? These patients had received wounds for which there was no prescribed medical treatment. There were ways to relieve the suffering of those whose death was inevitable, but we had no idea what to do with those who might pull through. We could operate on victims with broken bones or puncture wounds; but for burn cases all we could do was apply antiseptics, and there seemed to be no end to the fragments of glass, wood, and metal that had to be plucked out piece by piece from all over their bodies. As for the strange internal symptoms that gradually began to appear, there was nothing we could do but shake our heads and throw up our hands in despair.

One patient, for example, was having an excruciating time breathing. When I applied the stethoscope to his chest, I could hear a strange rattling noise every time he drew a breath. I could even hear a sound like someone stepping on broken glass. I immediately had an X-ray taken. When I looked at the developed film, I received yet another shock. I had thought that the wounds on his chest and back were simply cuts, but in fact glass shards and other unidentifiable objects had penetrated straight through into his lungs. How could such a thing possibly have happened? But more puzzling than the cause of his condition was the proper treatment: I simply did not have the slightest idea how I was going to remove so many foreign objects. Even with the advances made in chest surgery today, this would be an extremely difficult operation, and it would be untruthful to say that it was within my capacity.

And so I told the patient that he had contracted pneumonia and that though he would be uncomfortable for a day or two, the pain would gradually go away. I continued giving injections of morphine, and the next day he died. Such incidents occurred again and again, and my feelings of despair increased: "What is going to happen if we continue giving this kind of treatment? We have to get some experienced doctors here to help us."

I am sure that even the senior surgeons were feeling the same. Through the director of the hospital and high-ranking officers, we sent one telegraph after another for help to Kyushu University, Kurume University, and wherever else there were major hospitals. But we never received a reply from any of them. At first, we imagined ourselves in our patients' places and were extremely indignant, but on further reflection we realized that this lack of response was inevitable. All Japan was in a state of collapse, and those doctors probably could not have come even if they had wanted to; if in fact they had been able to travel anywhere, there were many places whose need for them was far greater than a fully equipped naval hospital. I found out later that at one treatment center it was all the staff could do to give each of the several hundred patients a drink of water once a day.

Once I knew that we could not expect reinforcements, I began to contact the Omura Airport barracks and regimental headquarters in an attempt to ascertain the physical nature of the "special bomb" and thus penetrate the causes of these mysterious symptoms. But whether this was classified information or they really did not know, the replies they gave me were almost no help at all. Since childhood I had liked physics, and I even knew a little about nuclear physics, but I did not yet realize that this had been an atomic bomb. I only found that out three or four days later. On the second day, all I could do was look on in great confusion and helplessness as my patients died.

Even those patients whose minds had functioned normally in spite of their great pain showed signs of clouded consciousness just before their deaths and often became delirious. "Doctor, doctor. See that swan swimming on the lake? Please call it here." "Oh, I dropped my handkerchief. Excuse me, but would you pick it up for me?" "How beautiful that fountain is!" Totally absorbed in their visions, they would utter these sorts of things while still unconscious. I realized at last that they were having hallucinations of whiteness. They often specifically mentioned white things, but even if they did not use the word white, the large percentage of what they said in their delirium was somehow related to whiteness.

Why were these dying victims of the atomic bomb possessed by hallucinations of whiteness? I cannot give the definitive answer, but I suspect that the violent flash of light when the bomb fell just before high noon had etched itself on their retinas and that this flash reappeared to them in hallucinations of whiteness just before they died. At least that is what, from my later studies of psychiatry, I believe happened.

Faced with the unrelenting suffering and inexorable death of our patients, we doctors, orderlies, and nurses all worked steadily around the clock without sleep or rest. On the fourth consecutive night without sleep, I was finally allowed to go to bed when doctors from the outlying cities came in to relieve us. I had continued to treat patients for four days and three nights since the explosion without sleeping.

Up until then I never even felt that I wanted sleep, partly out of a sense of responsibility, believing that it would be wrong to rest, and partly from extreme tension. But I was exhausted. Often I would even fall asleep while I was walking. Once I entered what I thought was Ward 8, looked around for a patient I was treating, and could not find him, only to discover that I had entered the wrong room. I had fallen fast asleep while I was walking and gone right past my own ward. While walking down the corridor, I would bump into someone. When I opened my eyes, I realized I had apologized to a post. This sort of thing happened to me not once but two or three times.

"Please Give Me a Comb . . . "

One of the most horrifying symptoms for the atomic bomb victims was the loss of hair. This symptom became apparent among some of our patients on the afternoon of the third day after their admission. I first learned about this condition from Iyonaga: "Something odd has just begun to happen. The patients' hair is falling out. All you have to do is touch it and it comes out in clumps. The same thing is happening to men and women."

As I hurried with him to their bedsides, the always considerate Iyonaga warned me that this condition had given the patients quite a shock and that I should conduct my examinations in as casual a manner as possible. The first patient I examined was a young girl of about twenty. She had not been critically injured and that morning had felt well enough to try to make herself a bit more presentable. At any rate, she had asked the nurse for a mirror and comb. No sooner had she touched the comb to her unkempt hair, which had not been tended to since the bombing, than the hair bunched into clumps and fell out. Heeding Iyonaga's advice, I walked in at a leisurely pace and approached the girl's bed as though making my ordinary rounds. "You seem much better today. Do you have a fever?" As I said this, I patted the girl on the top of her head where here and there patches of hair still remained. That instant the hair I touched all fell out. Startled, I instinctively drew my hand away. In an agonized voice, the girl asked, "Doctor, my hair is falling out. What is happening to me?" On the spot I invented a lie to tell her: "Loss of hair often accompanies burns," I said. "It should stop in a few days." I do not know whether she believed me or not. Two nights later she peacefully passed away. She had been a student at a women's college, but had been mobilized by the Women's Volunteer Corps to work in a Nagasaki munitions factory. She was quite a beautiful girl.

It soon became clear that loss of hair occurred in combination with several other symptoms. Usually, small purplish red spots appeared, accompanied by slight bleeding of the gums. Iyonaga asked me whether these were not cases of purpura hemorrhagica. I had too little experience to form any definite conclusions, but I did not believe that these were simple cases of purpura. When I checked with the other wards, all of them reported that similar symptoms had begun to appear in several of their patients as well.

There was another abnormal symptom that made me believe that these strange symptoms must have some connection with the bomb. We were injecting patients with glucose and a vitamin compound as a general precautionary measure to build up their strength. On some of the patients, however, the point of injection festered and turned a deep purplish color.

Normally, even if subcutaneous hemorrhaging occurs after an injection, most of the blood is absorbed by the next day. Not only had the hemorrhaging not been absorbed but putrefaction had gradually set in and the patients' condition was critical. Probably some abnormality had occurred in the blood itself and the blood vessels could not perform their normal functions. We immediately conducted a survey of all the patients we had admitted and discovered that more than thirty were bleeding from the gums, had purplish spots on their skin, and abnormal conditions around injection sites, while more than fifty were suffering from loss of hair.

From that point on the atmosphere in the hospital changed completely. Up until now the severely burned and injured had lapsed into critical condition and died one after another. Now we looked on helplessly as even those who at first glance seemed to have only minor injuries and were on the road to recovery were suddenly stricken. Loss of hair, dark purple skin after an injection, small spots like pin pricks appearing on the skin and gradually growing larger, bleeding from the gums—these were the telltale symptoms, and if they occurred in combination, we knew the patient would die.

Panic in the face of this new form of death reigned throughout the hospital. Patients repeatedly felt their hair, searched their arms and body for spots, checked their gums, stared at where they had received injections in abject terror. And the expression on their faces as their hair began to fall out! How many times did I catch sight of their inexpressible anguish as they held their breath and stared at the hair that had come off in their hands.

In my ward several young girls from the Women's Volunteer Corps had come to assist us. Though they had been in Nagasaki when the bomb fell, they had escaped without even a scratch. Their factories were now in ruins, and so they had bravely volunteered of their own free will to nurse their injured colleagues and fellow citizens. They worked diligently side by side with the Red Cross nurses. On these girls, too, those fatal signs began to appear.

"I feel so tired . . . I suppose I tried to do too much," they would say. "But it's for my country so I won't give up." Then they would notice that their own hair was coming out. There was no need to explain to them what was happening. No longer able to stand from fever and fatigue, they would collapse into beds in the very wards where they had been serving as nurses. These were girls from seventeen and eighteen to just around twenty. Unlike their contemporaries nowadays, they were very innocent and inexperienced. Death mercilessly struck them down nonetheless. Once the signs appeared, within two or three days at the earliest or ten days at the latest, they died without exception.

As the end approached, all of these girls, as if by common consent, asked for a comb. I suppose they wanted to give themselves one last grooming before they died. Most of their hair had fallen out, but in their dimmed consciousness they would repeatedly ask the nurses for a comb.

There were also girls who, as soon as they realized they were going to die, left their beds and used all their remaining strength to nurse others. As long as they had the strength to stand, they bravely determined to serve their fellow man. They were in constant attendance at the bedside of the critically injured, just the smell of whom was unbearable, and would even help them with their bedpans. How inspiring, how deeply moving was the sight of these dedicated girls!

One morning on my daily rounds, I came to the bed of one such girl who was lying with her eyes closed. "Good morning," I said to her with a specially cheerful voice. But she did not answer and showed no signs of being awake. When I tried to rouse her, I felt the characteristic limp heaviness of death. Her body was already cold. Her skin, with not a trace of make-up, was as translucent as white wax. Death had probably come to her in the middle of the night or just before dawn. It had come so quietly that no one had noticed her passing. How heartbreaking it must have been for her to die all alone with no one to tend her, with no one even knowing her final moment had come.

What the dying always wanted most from us doctors and nurses and orderlies was our hands. These hands of ours could not cure them or save them from death, but at least they could offer them the warmth of contact with a fellow human being. If we just held their

hands or put our hands on their foreheads as they lay
there staring at the ceiling mentally and physically exhausted, they would revive and smile at us. This was
particularly true just before they died. And so for a
time, our most important function was to hold our patients' hands. One patient, deliriously calling for her
father, gripped my hand so tightly it hurt. More than
thirty years later, I can still feel the pressure on my
fingers.

How much regret, how much resentment those
young girls must have felt, as they died helplessly,
without ever knowing the reason, from a mysterious
affliction brought on by the single blast of the atomic
bomb. As long as there is war, there is the risk of
death. These girls had sincerely believed in the war
effort. They had freely volunteered to work in factories
and hospitals for the good of their country.

Dressed in baggy *mompe* trousers and overalls made
out of a shabby-looking rayon material, they were far
removed from beauty in any ordinary sense of the
word. And yet to my mind they were incomparably
more beautiful physically and spiritually than the girls
who strut down the streets today in blue jeans or some
fashionable outfit. I wish that just once I could have
seen those girls dressed up in a miniskirt or an elegant
long dress, but they died with the end of the war only
moments away, never to know that such prosperity
would ever come to Japan.

These girls did not complain. But one word still
echoes in my ears: *kitsuka*. This is a Kyushu dialect
word to express unbearable pain. The only word of

complaint these girls ever uttered was this single word, *kitsuka*. Otherwise, they died keeping their regret and resentment to themselves.

The atomic bomb must not be elegized or sentimentalized, I have often asserted. It is not romantic fiction. It is not poetry. Its terrible workings and the devastation it wrought must be approached and described as scientifically as possible and viewed as a pressing concern of all mankind. But when I speak of these girls who died from atomic radiation, even now, in spite of myself my eyes grow wet with tears.

Performing Autopsies

To sum up simply yet intelligibly the intense radioactivity of the atomic bomb and its effects on the human body, radiation enters the body and invades the bone marrow and lymph glands. The body is unable to produce white blood cells, which are an important constituent of blood, and their number declines to as little as one tenth, one twentieth, or even less of their normal rate.

White blood cells perform various functions in the human body. Of special importance is their ability to destroy bacilli throughout the body by the process of suppuration. If the number of white blood cells decreases, however, bacilli are allowed to grow unchecked, suppuration does not occur, and instead all parts of the body begin to putrefy. Some of the symptoms of this process are festering where injections have been given, loss of hair, purplish spots on the skin, and bleeding from the gums.

We still did not know then that the "special bomb"

that had fallen on Nagasaki was the atomic bomb, but if we had known, I doubt that even the specialists would have realized the extent of its radioactivity. And, of course, it completely transcended the imagination of a novice doctor in training like myself.

In a few days, however, we were able to form some idea of the distinctive clinical features of the effects of radiation, the unknown disease we were battling. The first of these to emerge with numerical clarity as a result of blood tests was the decline in white blood cells. Patients who suffered from loss of hair or purpura symptoms invariably showed a significant decline, and at one point this decrease in the production of white blood cells occurred in me as well. My commanding officer, Lieutenant Commander Fukushima, mentioned that I was looking a bit tired. I assumed that it was only natural for me to be tired. The worst was now over and we no longer had to go four days and three nights without rest or sleep, but the working conditions in the hospital continued to be unabatedly arduous.

I replied that if I were tired, so was everyone else, but Lieutenant Commander Fukushima said that I did not look right and ordered me to have a blood test taken. Commander Fukushima is now dead, but he always regarded the men under him with a kind and fatherly eye. His sympathetic attention and kind heart led him to perceive that there was indeed something wrong with me.

Sure enough, when the blood test was taken, my white blood cell count had diminished dangerously.

The normal count is about six thousand per cubic millimeter, but my count was a mere three thousand. Ever since that first night, I had had continuous and direct contact with victims who had received high-level exposure to radioactivity, so it was inevitable that the radioactivity that they emitted would invade my own body, penetrate my bones, and attack my bone marrow. But as I have already mentioned many times, we did not then know how atomic radioactivity worked. At any rate, when the same decline in white blood cells appeared in me as in the patients who were losing their hair, I was considerably upset and my colleagues and superiors were very concerned for me.

There was no known way to cure the disease, yet the hospital could ill afford it if I were to stop being a doctor and become a patient. Nor had I any intention of letting that happen. I was overwhelmed with work and completely forgot about myself and everything else in my efforts to aid my patients in their peaceful progress toward death.

I was at least careful not to neglect building up my strength through the aid of injections of glucose and vitamin compounds. Fortunately my case was only in the initial stages, and my body accepted both intravenous and hypodermic injections without any festering around the injection sites. My physical stamina seems to have enabled me to win out over a secondary exposure to radiation. About ten days later, my white blood cell count had returned to normal, and I could for the time being breathe a sigh of relief. But what would have happened if my condition had not been noticed before it was too late? Whenever I think of that, I remember Commander Fukushima and his kind concern.

As these mysterious symptoms began to appear one after another with no means at our disposal to combat them and I myself was exposed to their danger, I became obsessed with the need to discover their true nature. There are two methods in pathology for studying the cause of an illness and its effects. One is to observe the condition in its acute stages. The other is to investigate the lingering symptoms when these have become chronic. Both of these methods are necessary to clarify the true nature of a disease, and no complete pathological conclusions can be drawn from one of these methods alone.

And so in addition to treating and tending the ill, I continued to record in minute detail the process of their deterioration. I asked a member of the photographic staff to take as many clinical photographs as possible. I myself had had some experience with photography before joining the service, and I borrowed a camera and constantly took pictures of my patients' horrifying deterioration. I also had a specialist take as many X-rays of them as possible.

But these steps by themselves were not enough. The most important data of all in pathology are tissue samples taken from the living or the dead. Almost every day, it seemed, scores of bodies were piled up to be buried in temporary graves. I was acutely aware of the need to perform autopsies on them before putrefaction set in and to extract their organs for analysis.

I was, however, fresh from medical school with only limited knowledge and experience and was not all that well versed in pathology. I did not believe that simply by performing these autopsies I could understand the true nature of the disease. That, I felt sure, would be made clear later, when experts finally came to the hospital. It *had* to be made clear. If it was not, then the souls of these people who had died so tragically could never rest in peace. That was why I wanted those samples. From the medical position, the one and only way that their deaths would not have been in vain was to preserve perpetually their tissue samples as testimony to the horrifying carnage in which they had died. It seemed to me that the voices of the dead were appealing to me to do so.

And so I asked Commander Fukushima for permission to perform postmortem examinations. For a naval hospital, this was a somewhat unprecedented request. The commander thought it over for a while, apparently considering various objections that the rest of the staff might raise, but he saw how earnest I was and gave me permission to conduct autopsies —if I did not do it too conspicuously.

I set off right away to find a place to work in. Omura Naval Hospital was a particularly well-equipped hospital even for the navy, but it did not have a postmortem room. And even if it had, I could not have used it. I could not use the operating rooms or sick bays either, of course. The patients' feelings had to be taken into consideration. I consulted with Iyonaga about whether there might be some inconspicuous place in which I could do postmortem examinations. Iyonaga mulled over the various rooms of the hospital that might serve this purpose and finally suggested the mortuary. "Hardly anyone ever goes in there, and it is filled with coffins which can be made into a dissecting table if we stack them up."

I had never been to the mortuary before and so had Iyonaga lead the way as I went to inspect it. Set a bit apart from the hospital wards was a small shed crudely constructed of wood. In the middle, as Iyonaga had said, were stacked many coffins hastily put together to accommodate the large number of corpses. I piled two coffins on top of one another, but this proved too low. Three was a bit too high, but I thought I could make do. I received permission from those in charge of handling the dead and promptly brought in dissecting equipment.

Before an autopsy can be performed, permission from the bereaved family is necessary. But we did not know the names or addresses of many of these dead, and even if we had, we did not know whether their relatives were dead or alive or how to get in touch with them. I was given permission to conduct autopsies on these dead as though they had no surviving relations.

There was one more hurdle to overcome—finding someone to assist me. All the orderlies and nurses were busy and tired to the point of exhaustion. None of them, moreover, wished to have any part in helping me. Their refusals were not on the grounds that dissections were a dirty, smelly job, but because they could see no point in them and did not feel they were worth the trouble. They were dedicated to helping the victims of injury or disease and these they nursed devotedly. What little free time they had, they would prefer to spend in the struggle to restore the living to health than in meddling with the dead. Such a preference was only natural for such dedicated professionals.

I resigned myself to the inconvenience and began to work alone. Iyonaga, however, was not able to stand idly by and agreed to assist me. Although we were working in different wards and it was extremely difficult for us to make the time, he helped me do the autopsies, even forgoing his sleep to do so.

The room was hot and stuffy when the blackout curtains were closed, for we were still on air raid alert. Under a dim light covered by a shade, we would lift a corpse onto the table made of coffins, say a prayer, then wield the scalpel. What horrific damage had been done to the tissue! As I made those incisions, how many times did I stifle a gasp or let out a sigh. Everywhere the veins had been torn to shreds, and the blood had seeped everywhere.

There were also numerous areas of hemorrhaging in the lungs and kidneys. But in addition to internal injuries of this nature, shards of glass and splinters of wood and metal, propelled by the force of the explosion, had penetrated the body, causing hemorrhaging in the lungs and abdomen. One by one I put the organs I extracted into cylindrical glass jars and preserved them in formaldehyde.

Day by day the number of these jars increased. At first we lined them up in a corner of our temporary postmortem room, but as the tempo of bringing in and taking out coffins increased, there was little room left for us to stand. Iyonaga set off to find an empty room. After making the rounds of the hospital's huge interior, at last he discovered an empty room that was hardly ever used. At one time it seems to have served as a storage room, and in fact from the looks of it, it should probably have been called a closet rather than a room. At any rate, it was just right for storing pathology samples.

Iyonaga and I would begin dissecting right after we had both gone off duty and keep it up, begrudging the time we needed for rest or sleep. To the inexperienced eye, these organs were merely grotesque lumps of flesh. But for us they were eloquent testimony to a horrible tragedy. Though we gasped and averted our eyes from the charred flesh and the puncture wounds with countless fragments of glass protruding from them, we felt an equally indescribable horror at the very sight of these organs. I seemed to hear each of them cry out to me: "Look at this!" "This is my ravaged body." "Who did this to me?" "Help!" "Don't let my death be in vain."

How many of these samples did we collect? Iyonaga and I did not stop to count but continued in silence, overwhelmed by the importance of our work.

Case Histories

On the morning of August 10, another large group of patients was brought in to Omura Naval Hospital. I provide below case histories of several who were in my charge. These records are excerpts from an article published in October 1945 under the title "Treatment of Nagasaki Atomic Bomb Victims and Findings of Their Postmortem Examinations." The content is slightly technical and may be hard to follow, but I have presumed to include it here in the hopes that the reader may understand more accurately the real and horrifying nature of radiation sickness.

Case 1   Factory worker, age 45, male
         Burns over entire body

Case 2   Student, age 19, female
         Explosion wounds on lower thighs (excessive
            bleeding)

Case 3   Student, age 17, female

Burns on face, left and right limbs, back, and right knee joint region. Contusions on right thigh

Case 4   Factory worker, age 29, male
Burns on neck and back region and on both upper limbs. Wounds in upper thighs from shell splinters and glass shards indirectly caused by the explosion

Case 5   Factory worker, age 30, male
Burns on back and both upper limbs

These five people were critically injured as a result of burns which covered their entire bodies or wounds from shell splinters indirectly caused by the bombing. All died within two or three days.

Case 6   Housewife, age 41, female
Burns on face and right upper limb. Contusions on lower limbs

At the time of the blast, this patient was within the circle five hundred meters in radius from the spot beneath the point of explosion. Since the bomb is estimated to have exploded five hundred meters above the ground, she is thought to have been one thousand meters away from the point of explosion. When admitted to the hospital, she was running a fever of about 38 degrees centigrade and showed symptoms of dysentery-like diarrhea and herpes-like ulcerations around the mouth. (Herpes is a skin disease marked by small virus-caused blisters.) A strange, foul smell clung to her, and on the morning of the thirteenth, her vision suddenly began to fade. At that time she remained lucid, but paralysis in her arms and legs began to set in and gradually intensified. On the morning of the fourteenth, signs of Kernig's symptom (an important symptom for diagnosing meningitis) and rigidity of the neck area appeared, and her consciousness faded. A lumbar puncture was immediately performed (a method to detect abnormalities in the cerebrospinal fluid), and dark red blood was found mixed with the spinal fluid. That afternoon her temperature rose to almost 40 degrees centigrade, and she was sweating profusely. She finally died that evening.

An autopsy was performed on her without delay. Patches of internal hemorrhaging ranging from a grain of rice to a pea in size were discovered here and there throughout the intestinal membrane. These were especially numerous in the rectum. In the other organs there were no major changes observable to the naked eye. In the brain, hemorrhaging was visible at the intersection of the middle and anterior cerebral artery and in the right ramus of the posterior cerebral artery, and blood clots had formed there. There were large cloudy regions on both sides of the temporal cortex. In addition, several blisterlike spots about as large as a grain of millet could be seen to have accumulated in areas the size of the tip of the little finger. Before the sudden change in her condition on the morning of the thirteenth, the patient had had a high temperature but no neurological symptoms. Consequently, the brain hemorrhaging could not have been the result of an ordinary external wound but is thought to have been caused by thrombosis brought on by high-intensity burns or some other forms of arteritis.

Case 7   Factory worker, age 19, male
             Burns on right upper limb and left lower thigh

This patient was about one thousand meters from the hypocenter when the bomb fell. His wounds were not all that serious, and he responded satisfactorily to treatment and was released from the hospital on the fifteenth. About two weeks later, however, we learned that back in his hometown he had started to run a fever, suffered from loss of appetite, general lassitude, loss of hair, subcutaneous hemorrhaging, and loose, bloody stools, and he had subsequently died. There have been many similar cases.

Case 8   Student, age 17, female
             Burns on back and left lower limb

It is estimated that this girl was 1,200 to 1,300 meters from the hypocenter. When admitted to the hospital, she had a temperature of 40 degrees centigrade, awful sores around the mouth, and foul-smelling breath. The impairment of her vision gradually increased, and finally brain fever set in. From the eleventh, purpura-like patches of subcutaneous hemorrhaging became visible on the skin of her arms and legs. By the fourteenth, these patches had spread over her body and ranged from about the size of a grain of rice to the size of a thumb. A blood test showed a count of 1.5 million red blood cells per cubic millimeter (the average for a healthy body is 4 million), 300 white blood cells (a healthy average is from 4,000 to 5,000), and hemoglobin of 31 percent (80–90 percent in a healthy body). A cerebrospinal tap revealed exactly the same findings as in Case 6. The patient died late on the night of the fifteenth.

The postmortem examination revealed blood clots about the size of a grain of rice beneath the mucous membrane throughout the small intestine. There was also hemorrhaging in one section of the arteries in the forehead, and spots in the cerebral membrane similar to those found in Case 6 were everywhere throughout the anterior lobe.

Case 9   Child, age 9, male
          Contusions on scrotum

This victim was also about one thousand meters from the hypocenter when the bomb fell. On the eleventh, the patient contracted a fever which then began to escalate. His wound was only one millimeter deep, and there had been almost no bleeding from it. Although there were no other injuries which could account for it, on the fourteenth his hair began to fall out in patches all over his head. With a mere touch of the fingers, it would fall out with no resistance and stick to the fingertips. On the fifteenth, patches of subcutaneous hemorrhaging and the characteristic ulcerations around the mouth started to spread. The groin wound showed no signs of healing, and on the evening of the sixteenth he died.

Several other patients showed exactly the same

symptoms. Blood transfusions, vitamin compounds, hypertonic glucose solutions, hormones, and special drugs to stop hemorrhaging were given, but the patients' condition only deteriorated and each died in turn. Most of these patients had only minor injuries. The very few who had more extensive injuries were not in critical condition and had recovered, only to become sick again much later. The following case is an extreme example of this phenomenon.

Case 10   Student, age 14, male
          No external wounds except a five-millimeter
          scratch on the lower lip

This patient was within about one thousand meters of the bomb's hypocenter, but fortunately escaped injury. After the bombing, he seemed perfectly healthy and was able to help around the house and perform other tasks. But on the twentieth he began to run a fever, his hair fell out, and other such symptoms started to appear. He was admitted to the hospital on the twenty-fourth and died on the morning of the twenty-fifth.

His physique and development at the time of admission were about normal, but he was undernourished, his face flushed and emaciated.

temperature	39.4° C
pulse	120 per minute
pupil reaction to light	sluggish
tongue	covered with dry brownish fur

mucous membrane/	
pharynx	reddish
tonsils	enveloped in whitish fur
lips	swollen, especially around the wound on the lower lip, which had worsened

In addition, the lymph glands beneath the jaw had swollen to the size of the tip of the index finger, and the patient complained of oppressive pain. Subcutaneous hemorrhaging was visible in spots all over his body, and there was a conspicuous loss of hair. He complained that his heart raced spasmodically, and his breathing was harsh.

A postmortem examination was made four hours after death. The outer membrane of the heart and the exterior surface of both lungs showed signs of clotting and hemorrhaging. The liver was a slimy dark purplish red on the surface, but when cut open was transparent, and the lobular structure was a little indistinct. The spleen was slightly smaller than usual, but there was no apparent softening. Nothing seemed wrong with the kidneys, but the left side of the renal pelvis was filled with blood clots, though no injury to the white matter was apparent.

In the adrenal glands, there were no changes in the medulla, cortex, or adipose tissue, but there were a few surface blood clots both right and left. There were no apparent changes in the pancreas. The mucous membrane of the digestive tract and stomach revealed several blood clots ranging from the size of a grain of millet to the size of a soybean. There was blood clotting on the large and small intestines and the upper diaphragm. Nothing unusual was observed in the bladder.

Let me restate these findings in statistical form and examine the results. These ten victims of the atomic bomb blast at Nagasaki all died with a predisposition to hemorrhaging.

1. Noticeable clotting on the outer membrane of each organ and beneath the mucous membrane

    observed to extend from the esophagus to the rectum .... 8 cases

    only in the intestines .... 6 cases

    only in the large intestine .... 2 cases

    only in the rectum .... 2 cases

    observed in the spleen, kidneys, etc. .... 8 cases

    hemorrhaging only in the brain and in no other organ .... 1 case

2. White spots on the mucous membrane of the large intestine .... 3 cases

3. Hemorrhaging in the vessels at the base of the brain .... 6 cases

4. Ruptures in the organs

    ruptured liver .... 3 cases

    ruptured spleen .... 2 cases

    ruptured lungs .... 2 cases

5. Bone marrow dissolved into pale yellowish red .... 1 case

From the above observations and other data, the victims of the atomic bomb at Nagasaki can be broadly divided into four categories: (1) those instantaneously disintegrated by the force or radiant heat of the blast or those who were vaporized by it (not the object of medical analysis); (2) burn cases; (3) those with wounds caused indirectly by the explosion; (4) those who fell ill with predisposition to hemorrhaging (these patients are divided into two groups: those who fell ill immediately after the disaster with the symptom of dysenteric diarrhea and those who fell ill after a latency period). Of these four categories, the first obviously cannot be the subject of medical investigation. Likewise, patients in the second and third categories are only at issue when they also fall into the fourth category. Consequently, that category is of greatest significance. Let us investigate it in more detail.

GENERAL OUTLINE OF CASES
SHOWING A PREDISPOSITION TO HEMORRHAGING
AMONG ATOMIC BOMB VICTIMS AT NAGASAKI

Cause: Presumed to be damage caused by radiant heat or radiation produced by nuclear fission.

Latency Period: In general, in direct proportion to the distance from the source of the explosion. Two of the seventy-one people assumed to have been within 750 meters of the explosion showed symptoms on that same day, while symptoms appeared four days later in six people who were within about 1,000 meters of the source of the explosion. Symptoms were noticed about ten days later among those who were thought to have been between 1 and 1.5 kilometers from the blast. Thirty people who had received no injuries whatsoever at the time of the explosion were admitted twenty to twenty-five days after the bombing complaining of symptoms of radiation poisoning. All of these people had been on the periphery or outside of the area 1.5 kilometers from the blast.

CONDITION I: NO COMPLICATIONS

Suddenly overcome by general lassitude, loss of appetite, and a fever that escalates as high as 40 degrees centigrade. Mild swelling of the lymph glands throughout the body, especially in the neck. After one or two days, loose, slimy, bloody stools, blood in the urine, and loss of hair. Subcutaneous hemorrhaging appears on the limbs and trunk, at first about the size of a pinprick but growing within a few days to the size of a grain of rice or a pea. Bleeding from the mucous membrane in the oral cavity and characteristic herpeslike mouth sores appear. As death approaches, these become gangrenous and start to spread. The characteristic foul-smelling breath worsens.

There is no conspicuous damage to the heart or the circulatory system, but as the end approaches the blood pressure plummets. Because of high fever or general weakening perhaps, a pneumonialike condition is apt to occur. During this period, the body temperature continues to rise. In the final stages, the patient registers the highest temperature; then suddenly it falls and the patient dies. Some patients suffer severe vision disabilities and some receive brain damage. Victims who did not experience brain damage suffered no clouding of consciousness. In fact, in spite of their high fevers, most of them were extremely calm and lucid.

Results of urinalysis showed albumin and urobirinogen (a symptom that appears with malfunctioning of the liver). Blood tests gave the following results.

	Atomic Bomb Victims	*Normal*
red blood cells	1–2 million	4 million
white blood cells	2–5 hundred	4–5 thousand
hemoglobin	30–50%	80–90%
bleeding time	20 min.–2 hr.	1–3 min.

CONDITION II: COMPLICATED BY SURFACE WOUNDS

In general, most of the people who suffered from the characteristic symptoms detailed in Condition I had sustained minor wounds. Very few had severe burns. Until Condition I manifested itself, granulation had taken place and other aspects of the healing process seemed to be occurring normally, but as the end approached a gangrenous condition spread around the surface of the wound, emitting a foul smell.

Prognosis: As of September 10, everyone showing these symptoms has died.

Diagnosis: Very easily recognized from the symptoms and case histories detailed above.

Treatment: Hypertonic glucose solutions, massive injections of vitamins C, B, and K, blood transfusions, and hormone injections have been tried but absolutely without success except in the most minor cases.

Additional Remarks: No notable differences in the way the disease affects men and women.

Of the approximately twenty thousand patients admitted and treated as of September 10, only three suffered from tetanus. None had received antitetanus serum in advance. But though undoubtedly there was both danger of tetanus from the nature of their wounds and the opportunity to contract it while in the streets or on the trains that carried them to the hospital, I believe it is a fact worth recording that so few did contract the disease.

The War Comes to an End

August 15. This day too the sky was clear and the midsummer sun shone like a blazing fire overhead. On reflection, I realized that every day since the ninth when the bomb had fallen, the scorching sun had continued to shine, except during that one period of black rain.

We were informed of the war's end, as were most civilians, by the emperor's radio broadcast, but I felt no emotion whatsoever as I listened. When I had seen the piles of bomb victims carried in by truck on that first night I had thought to myself, "The war is over." There were two reasons for my belief. First, the enemy had developed an instrument of mass destruction that surpassed imagination and had dropped it first on Hiroshima and then on Nagasaki. Now that Japan had completely lost control of the air, what would happen if such a weapon were dropped on more of its cities, one after another? I could only conclude that the end of the war was a matter of time.

My other reason was the horrifying effects of this weapon, the callousness and cruelty that could instantaneously send so many human lives into a veritable hell. Could this form of man's inhumanity to man ever be allowed to happen again? If such carnage were to continue, the ultimate result could only be the destruction of the human race and the devastation of the earth. This was the end of war as we had known it. I did feel some relief that the war was over. Primarily I was relieved because the third city designated for atomic destruction had been spared; and also because from now on I could go about treating patients and performing autopsies under bright lights instead of the dimmed illumination of the blackout period.

Almost all the army and naval units were preparing to disband and demobilize, but the war was not over for us. Today as yesterday, most of the patients were gasping in pain. Today as yesterday, loss of hair and hemorrhaging occurred, forcing the victims to their inescapable deaths.

About five o'clock that evening there suddenly came an order for all hands to assemble. We were concerned about leaving our patients, but in obedience to this order from the hospital's director, we left them in the care of the minimum number of emergency personnel and gathered in the open space to the west of the hospital compound. The officers were in the very first row, and so we doctors in training lined up with them. It was announced that a burning of the emperor's portrait was about to take place.

First, as everyone saluted, the navy flag was low-

ered. Then we continued saluting as the imperial portrait was to be burned. The method chosen to burn
it seemed inappropriate somehow, and we could only
look at one another and wonder what on earth was
going on.

The director of the hospital had prepared several
bottles of alcohol. He ordered a subordinate to pour
one on the glass frame which held the imperial portrait and then set fire to it with a match. This only
caused the alcohol to burn, however; the frame itself
did not catch fire. A stiff breeze was blowing in from
Omura Bay, and the midsummer sun as it set was so
dazzling we could not even see the flames.

When this alcohol burned off, the director had
another bottle poured over the portrait and another
match lit. If he had used gasoline, the portrait would
have burned at once, but instead he had the same procedure repeated again and again, dozens of times. We
continued standing at attention and saluting. The
Japanese salute was made by raising the right arm
horizontally, bending the elbow and bringing the finger tips near to the brim of the military cap. Unlike
the easy salute of the U.S. military, the Japanese
salute required the full strength of the body. If made to
sustain such a salute in the hot sun over a long period,
it would be odd indeed if some did not faint from exhaustion.

The midsummer sun as it went down beneath
Omura Bay was remarkably hot, and the collars and
backs of our uniforms were drenched with sweat. As expected, a fellow doctor in training beside me crumpled

and fell. To the right of me, another colleague staggered and collapsed. Orderlies came running up and carried the men who had fainted into the hospital.

In spite of this, the director did not desist in his attempt to burn the imperial portrait by the odd method he had selected. Perhaps he had too much respect for the emperor's portrait and felt it was in the true national spirit to take a long time to burn it.

The next two and one-half hours passed without the order to stand at ease being given. The director of the hospital was still burning alcohol. The sun had almost set. My arm and fingers were numb, and there was no sensation in them whatsoever. I propped my left hand under my right arm and tried desperately to hold myself together, but my wits were dulled and even the concern for my patients which had been troubling me until just moments earlier faded from my consciousness. When I came to again, almost all the officers had disappeared. I assume they had fainted and been carried away.

After the sun had finally disappeared, the director gave up his original purpose and ordered someone to run off and get some gasoline. As black smoke and red flames flickered in the twilight, he ordered an end to our eccentric salute of two and one-half hours.

I may seem to have spent too much time relating an incident that has no direct relation to the atomic bombing of Nagasaki, but I have included it here because I believe it casts some light on the hospital director's odd behavior toward my pathology samples a few days later. I will discuss this further in the next chapter.

Here I would like to take the opportunity to record what Nagasaki looked like as I saw it with my own eyes right after the war ended.

I felt strongly that in order to grasp its true nature, I needed to visit the scene of the disaster as soon as possible. But the pressure of work made it impossible to find time for such a visit, and so it was not until after the war had ended that my wish was finally fulfilled. I was given a round-trip ticket between Omura Station and Nagasaki Station, but I only had a one-day leave.

From military information and patients' descriptions, I had constructed in my mind some impression of what the site would look like, but as the train approached the center of Nagasaki, I could only stare in astonishment at devastation that made all my worst expectations insignificant by comparison. I alighted from the train and, relying on a map, began to make as wide a tour of the area as possible. As far as the eye could see, everything had been reduced to burned-out ruins. This was true not only of the area where the bomb had actually fallen. In all directions, buildings had been flattened and burned to the ground. Even reinforced concrete buildings had collapsed like crushed paper boxes. Thick girders cut into the earth as though they had been hammered into place.

The blast of the explosion had not spread uniformly out from the center. In certain areas it seemed to have acted like a cyclone. In one block, for example, half of the buildings had collapsed toward the east while the other half had fallen to the west. Even where the exterior shell of stone buildings remained intact, their interiors were littered with rubble as though some giant had run amuck inside.

I wrote earlier that paper piled in a storehouse had all been incinerated by the bomb's heat. This was the day I observed that phenomenon. From the name plate that still hung on the charred gate post, I realized that the complex had been a paper mill. As I approached what was left of the warehouse, I was astonished to see that all the paper still piled mountain high had turned to ashes. I picked up a steel rod lying nearby and thrust it into the pile, but it pierced to the center, meeting no resistance whatsoever.

At any rate, the heat of the bomb certainly defied the imagination: the leaves of the trees on the mountains within eighty kilometers in all directions had been burned off, the trees looking as bare and desolate as though it were late autumn instead of midsummer.

One big factory had employed about ten thousand workers. When it tried to rebuild after the bombing, there were fewer than one hundred people able to undertake clearance operations. About half of them, who at first glance seemed perfectly well, suffered from loss of hair and hemorrhaging, and they too died.

The policemen I met on my inspection tour and people at military-related establishments adamantly asserted that the damage had been greatest at places which received the direct light of the sun. There is a counterargument to this, however. The explosion took place at 11:02 A.M. when the sun was almost directly overhead. In other words, *all* locations were receiving the direct light of the sun. Unless you were indoors at the time, everyone and everything encountered exactly the same conditions. Consequently, the sun's rays themselves were not the catalytic agent, but perhaps places which admitted ample sunshine were particularly susceptible to the blast and heat and radiation of the bomb.

Be that as it may, many people who were in direct physical contact with something metal—those wearing wristwatches or carrying lunch pails, for example—received particularly severe burns in those areas and were likely to show symptoms of radiation sickness later on. Likewise, burns were said to be especially serious on those who were wearing black clothes, while people who wore white escaped with only minor burns. One of the patients I treated had been wearing a black and white striped shirt and had actually received burn wounds in stripes. Clinical results showed, however, that these observations held true only of places that were more than two kilometers from the hypocenter and where the effects of the bomb were relatively mild. Nearer where the bomb fell, it made no difference whether one was wearing white or black.

The long day at last came to an end, and I arrived back at Omura Station. Somewhere or other I had a late lunch, but I had no recollection of where or what I had eaten. When I returned late to the hospital, a meal was laid out in the officers' room with a napkin over it and a name tag with my name on it.

My Pathology Samples
Are Thrown Away

Our patients' suffering and terror of death remained unchanged with the ending of the war, and we were kept busy treating and tending them. Iyonaga and I, in particular, were incredibly busy with the important business of postmortem examinations.

Several days after the war had ended, I was awakened early one morning from a light sleep by a violent pounding on my door. I heard Iyonaga's voice calling me. I rubbed my eyes and answered him. He opened the door and came rushing in with totally unexpected news. All the pathology samples that we had kept in the room we referred to as our "depository" had disappeared! Astonished, I leaped out of bed. "All of them?" I asked. "Every single one," he replied. This was a shock. Who had taken our precious samples and when? Iyonaga continued his report.

"I too was surprised and asked the staff member in charge. According to him, late last night all the samples were dumped out on the hill behind the hospital by order of the director." "The hospital director?" I asked. "But why?" Iyonaga had no idea.

What was going on? The director of the hospital, upon graduating from the medical school of the University of Tokyo with an outstanding record, had entered the navy and advanced to the rank of rear admiral. As a student of Dr. Kunihiko Hashida, the acknowledged authority in physiology in those days (he became minister of education after the war), the director must have had considerable expertise in physiology. No one could have known better than he the significance and value of those pathology specimens. Why had he ordered someone to throw away those precious specimens of radiation sickness, and in the middle of the night at that?

I immediately recalled how the director looked on the evening that the war ended, when he made all of us stand at attention and salute for two and one-half hours. And I finally understood what Commander Fukushima had meant when he advised me not to be too conspicuous with my autopsies.

Those samples did not belong to me alone, however. In them resided the suffering of all the many victims who had died from the bomb. They could not be so lightly dismissed, so easily discarded as that. I felt impelled to ask the director for an explanation and demand that justice be done. I am sure Iyonaga felt the same way. But like the good soldier that he was, he showed no emotion but simply said in a businesslike way, "I will take someone with me and go look for the samples." And he hurried off.

I put my clothes on and headed for the director's office. In the normal order of things, the difference in rank between a rear admiral and a doctor in training was like night and day. Any request from below had to go through several intermediate stages before it ever reached his attention. I cast such caution to the winds and charged right into the director's office. Though the imperial proclamation had declared an end to the war, I was still in the navy and as long as I remained there might be subject to punishment for such insubordination, but I resolved to face that possibility when I came to it.

Trying to push aside the aide-de-camp who was blocking my way, I demanded an explanation from the director. He answered me quietly, showing no signs of discomposure or annoyance: "Japan has been defeated. What is the point of scholarship?" That was all he said. As I think about it now, perhaps that was how he really felt. As a soldier who had dedicated his entire life to his country, he had nothing left once the country was defeated in war. Scholarship and research were worthless; even the fact the Japanese people had survived no doubt did not enter into his consideration. But the person who is really human, I believe, is the one who reads books and disciplines his mind right up to the moment of death. In all ages and all lands, many stories continue to be told of people who refused to abandon their studies though confined to jail or subjected to political oppression. Even without carrying the argument that far, there was no reason for him to have gone to such lengths as to throw away what another person had worked so hard to accomplish. All I could do was grit my teeth and say:

"Sir, what connection can there possibly be between Japan's defeat and medical science? Why is it wrong to record for medical purposes these unfortunate events so that they may never happen again? I believe these records are most important, not only for the Japan of the future but for all the peoples of the world. And if we do not make these records and carry out these autopsies, how can we possibly justify our behavior to our patients who are dying in agony?"

The director of the hospital, as well as his aide-de-camp and secretary who happened to be there at the time, must have been surprised by this impassioned plea from such an impudent young man. But the director was a mature person. He did not get angry or offer any counterarguments, nor did he insist on his own way. He kept stonily silent while the expression on his face said, "Do as you please."

I left the director's office and raced to the hill behind the hospital. Iyonaga and several soldiers were engaged in recovery operations. When he saw me, he asked with some concern what had happened with the director. "He seems to have acquiesced," I replied. "Then we can go on with the autopsies?" "We will go on with them even if he is opposed." "Good," Iyonaga said, and for the first time he looked relieved.

"Look at this, Dr. Shiotsuki. The samples have all been carefully treated. Even though it was the director's orders, the soldiers assigned to throw the samples out seem to have understood how you felt." I looked around and saw that all the glass containers with the samples in them had been carefully placed on a patch of grass. If these containers had been unceremoniously tossed out, all of our efforts so far would have been smashed with them, and the organs of those who had died of acute radiation poisoning would have been lost once and for all. I was deeply grateful to the men for showing so much consideration.

Although it was midsummer, the coldness of the ground and the dew on the grass during the night and early morning had preserved the specimens from change. Nevertheless since it had been the middle of the night when the soldiers had thrown the samples out and they could not see clearly what they were doing, the caps of several containers had come loose and dirt had gotten insde. We carefully washed the dirt off and replaced the specimens in a fresh solution of formaldehyde.

We were able to collect almost all the discarded samples, but our next concern was where to put them. I did not relish returning them to the empty room that we had been using as our depository. That might be interpreted as direct defiance of the director, and then all our efforts really would come to an end. All of us, soldiers included, put our heads together to think of a good hiding place. Relieved at having managed to collect most of the specimens, someone joked that when he was a young boy, he used to be good at hiding his piggy bank.

The containers were bulky, and there were so many of them. Someone had the bright idea of hiding them under the beds. The enlisted men's quarters would not do, but I had a private room where the samples could be hidden. It was a good suggestion, but there were just too many containers for all of them to fit. Someone else had a suggestion: "This hospital is constructed differently from others. If you loosen the paneling, there is quite a bit of space between it and the outer walls." This was a brilliant observation. We hurried to the small hut cum mortuary and loosened the paneling. The space was just large enough to serve as a hidden cupboard for the containers. We were so pleased with our discovery that for the first time since the bomb had fallen we were able to smile once again.

Leaving Omura Hospital

The month of August came to an end. Half a month had passed since the end of the war. American troops were stationed throughout the country, and Japanese forces were being disbanded. Demobilization of almost all units had been completed, and ex-soldiers were returning home from overseas.

Demobilization had begun at Omura Naval Hospital as well. There were still many patients there, but doctors from Nagasaki and adjoining prefectures came in to replace us, and we were relieved of our duties and allowed to return home. As a general rule, people whose homes were the farthest away were demobilized first, and since I came from Tokyo my turn came fairly quickly. But I pretended I had not received orders and continued to stay where I was. Iyonaga was from Fukuoka so his demobilization would inevitably be rather late, and we could continue with our autopsies as before. Medical treatment still proved of no avail, and patients continued to die. Of course, there were people who recovered and left the hospital; on the other hand, there seemed to be no end to the numbers of critically ill patients brought in to us from other treatment centers throughout the prefecture.

But as we entered September and one day passed after another, I began to feel uneasy about my position, oppressed by the uncertainty of when I would be forced to leave. One of the noncommissioned officers in charge of settling remaining affairs, with an almost tearful expression, once begged me: "I understand how you feel, but your presence is complicating the demobilization process, and we would really appreciate it if you would leave." I continued to hold out by saying that there were five or six patients whose progress I was particularly concerned about and did not want to leave until their condition stabilized.

But finally I was driven into a position where I was no longer allowed to do as I pleased. Just before noon on September 14, a peremptory command came in for Lieutenant Shiotsuki. (It had been decided that in spite of the end of the war our certificates of graduation from the old imperial universities would be issued as planned on September 25, and that we would be given the rank of lieutenant junior grade. This seemed to have something to do with our separation pay as well.) The contents of the message read: "Lieutenant Shiotsuki is instructed to leave the premises and demobilize with all due speed tomorrow, September 15. Wages and separation pay may be claimed today prior to 1500 hours (3 P.M.)."

I assumed that the hospital director had decided to chase me out of the hospital. He had the ultimate responsibility for the final settling of affairs. The official reason, however, was that the occupation by U.S. troops had been stepped up, and in order to avoid unnecessary friction, only the minimum necessary military personnel were to remain. Orders had come for all other personnel to withdraw as rapidly as possible. Against such orders no protest was possible.

The demobilization orders had come very suddenly, but if I refused to obey them and tried to stay at my post, I would probably be thrown out bodily. I had no choice but to start packing. Various provisions such as rice, sugar, and hardtack, which were kept in great quantities in storehouses on the hill behind the hospital, were distributed to demobilized soldiers according to their rank. Included as well was a large military duffle bag to carry the supplies in.

Human selfishness, which is all too apt to raise its ugly head on such occasions, inevitably revealed itself at Omura. People showed all sorts of surprising enterprise and craftiness in finding ways to take just a bit more than they were entitled to. I heard that one of the senior officers, conspiring with someone in the air corps, had managed to load a truck not only with foodstuffs but even with fuel, drive to the airport, present forged copies of the necessary orders, and fly off for no-one-knows-where. At about the same time, a high-ranking officer is said to have made off with all of the latest model microscopes which had been brought in by submarine from Germany and were being kept at Omura Naval Hospital.

To tell the truth, I too wanted to take as much food and clothing as I possibly could, since I would be returning to Tokyo, which had been reduced to burned rubble in the war. But there was something else I wanted to take with me even more—the pathology samples I had collected during the past month.

By rights they belonged to Omura Naval Hospital and as hospital property should be handed over as research material, no matter whether the hospital was turned over to the public domain or requisitioned by the occupation forces. But because the hospital director who had ordered the specimens thrown out would remain until such a transfer was made, I despaired of the specimens' fate. I was overwhelmed by a sense of uncertainty about what would happen to them if I did not take them with me.

My discharge papers had come through so quickly that I would have no time to pack the specimens or even make the necessary arrangements for their shipment. I checked with Omura Station, but soon realized from the confused state of the railroad shipping office that it would be impossible. "All right," I grimly resolved, "I will carry them on my own back, no matter how heavy they are!" I had one extremely good piece of luck. Iyonaga's discharge had come through on the same day as mine. He was going to his home in Fukuoka, but he promised to carry as many specimens as he could and help me when I changed to the main train line. I immediately cheered up and calculated that I could take at least fifty specimen bottles with me.

After collecting my separation pay and settling other necessary business, I made my last official tour of my ward, then rushed to put the specimens in order. All of them were in fragile glass containers. I would have to protect them by wrapping them in something as thick as possible, but there were not even old newspapers in the hospital for me to use. I hurried around to the dispensary and the kitchen and collected paper, sacks, cardboard boxes, anything that could be used for packing. Then I laid out all the clothes I would not actually be wearing the next morning, from white shirts down to my underwear.

Not only Iyonaga but other members of the unit volunteered to help sort and pack the specimens. I was deeply grateful for their assistance. They were dedicated right up to the very end. If it had not been for their help, I am sure I would never have completed the packing in time. While the packing operations were under way, I went around to the various departments and collected the case histories and X-rays connected with the specimens. More than anything else though, I wanted a microscope, for without one it would have been impossible to continue my research.

Actually in my student days I had owned the latest model German microscope. My father had found it and some German medical texts, which were quite difficult to obtain in those days. When I entered the navy, I entrusted these precious possessions through a friend to the safekeeping of the Swiss embassy. The thought that I might die in the war had weighed on my mind, and I left a will instructing that if anything were to happen to me, these articles were to be donated to a student who loved learning.

I knew that the Swiss embassy would return the microscope to me if it could, but my real fear was that it might not have survived the war intact. Tokyo had been the object of repeated bombings, and I could not help thinking that my microscope had already been destroyed. Then I spotted a Zeiss microscope that belonged to the hospital. It was not as new or as good as the ones that that high-ranking officer had made off with during the confusion, but if I had this microscope I could continue my research without impediment. I relinquished my share of provisions and instead received this microscope, going through the proper channels.

Packing operations proceeded, with all of us working through the night. The problem that most concerned me was what to do about the remaining specimens. Firmly believing that these specimens should not be destroyed and that one day they would be studied by specialists, I pasted labels with all the pertinent data on each container and put them back—not in the empty space behind the paneling but lined up in rows on the shelves of the depository. This job was the one that actually took the most time. Day was just dawning when I finally finished putting everything in order.

After that I took a brief nap and then ate a hearty breakfast. To carry my heavy pack was going to require considerable stamina, and I was resolved to make the necessary preparations for the ordeal ahead.

I put the duffle bag packed full of specimens on my back like a rucksack and carried specimens and other belongings in both hands. These other belongings included the microscope I mentioned earlier and a sword inscribed with the name of its maker, the famous Masamune. This was a valuable heirloom worth a great sum even in those days, and I could not conceivably leave it behind. Finally there was the box lunch invariably given to each person in the navy as he hit the road. This was all I took with me when I left.

Because I was an officer or perhaps because I was such a confounded nuisance that they wanted to get rid of me as soon as possible, I was fortunate enough to be driven to Omura Station with Iyonaga and all our baggage. Just before the car was about to arrive, I visited Ward 8 for the last time. I had already been relieved of my duties, so this was not a sick round. It was my last expression of sympathy to my patients and a quiet leave-taking. The patients, as always, were lying in their beds. Some were gasping in pain; others were sleeping peacefully.

The emotion I felt as I said a reluctant goodbye to these people, whom I had been tending until now with everything in my power, is something that only another doctor can understand. With patients on the road to recovery, saying goodbye is simply a matter of time, since all of them will eventually leave the hospital one day. But almost all these patients were still hovering between life and death. No one knew when those mysterious symptoms would suddenly appear and drag another victim to the abyss. Or perhaps after I had gone some new syndrome would occur that might prove fatal. I had to desert these people, desperately dependent on their doctor, trembling with dread at what might happen next. How could I say goodbye to them? How could I tell them that as of that day I was being discharged from the service?

There was one nineteen-year-old girl from the Women's Volunteer Corps whose face had been badly burned. "Doctor, can't you do something about my face? Please fix it, doctor, please." I had heard this heartrending appeal of hers many times. Her entire face had been charred reddish black, her eyebrows were gone, and her nose and lips were totally disfigured. Her eyes alone shone with their original beauty. There was nothing I could do for her. "How have you been?" I asked. "You're looking better." And casually I patted her on the shoulder and clasped her hand. Her hand had not been burned and was long and narrow, like a silver fish—both beautiful and elegant. Don't give up. Please don't give up. Go on living. Silently I pleaded with her in my heart.

Radiation symptoms had already appeared in the next patient and his hair had begun to thin. Pretending to check his temperature, I put my hand to his forehead and silently bade him farewell. And so I said a quiet goodbye to all my patients. Almost all the military doctors and orderlies had been replaced by civilians, and only the dedicated Red Cross nurses still remained.

Iyonaga came in and whispered that the car had come. I left the ward feeling as though I was leaving a

part of my heart behind there. As the car carrying
Iyonaga and me and the pathology samples was about
to pass through the gates, the few orderlies who remained lined up and waved goodbye with their caps
in the traditional naval farewell. I waved my own hat
out of the car window to the soldiers who had come to
see me off and to my patients in Ward 8.

The gate receded into the distance and my ward
with it, but I continued to lean out of the window and
wave my cap over and over again until the hill where
the hospital stood had completely disappeared from
view.

My Long Journey
with the Pathology Samples

From Omura Station I went to Hakata, then transferred to a train heading east. This train took me to Nagoya, and from there I headed to Karuizawa, a resort village about 150 kilometers from Tokyo, where my family was. My father had died before I entered the service, and my mother and younger sister had fled from Tokyo and settled in Karuizawa. The ultimate destination for me and my specimens, however, was my alma mater, Tohoku University. But before going there I would need to reorganize them once again and, besides, I wanted to let my mother and sister know that I was all right. And so I made my way to Karuizawa.

Even though it was mid-September, nights in Kyushu were still hot and humid. The sun had already started to set when I arrived in Hakata, but the platform was sultry with the heat. The train originating from Hakata seemed to have just pulled into the platform, but almost all the seats were already taken, although there was still room in the aisle. Fortunately I found an empty seat next to the aisle, and with Iyonaga's help was able to put the sample containers under the seat and in the aisle beside me.

The person in the seat next to me was a navy man, and I realized from his collar badges that he was a commander in the navy air corps. The moment I had stowed my belongings away and was breathing a sigh of relief, our eyes happened to meet. Automatically I sprang to attention, saluted, and then settled down in my seat.

Just then the aisles began to fill with demobilized personnel, and I urged Iyonaga to get off the train while there was still time. For more than a month, ever since the bomb fell on Nagasaki, we had worked diligently together, forgetting to eat and sleep, as we pursued our research and tended the injured. We would probably have many opportunities to meet again, but now that it was time to say goodbye a flood of emotion pressed in upon me. As departure time approached, the train was jampacked. The crowd of people blocked my last view of Iyonaga, standing there on the platform.

Soon the train began to move. The commander in the seat beside me asked me where I was coming from. When I told him that I had been at Omura Naval Hospital, he told me in a friendly way that he had been in the air corps at Omura. He asked me about the baggage I was carrying, and when I told him that it contained the organs of atomic bomb victims and described briefly the aims of my postmortem examinations, he listened with an expression of profound emotion on his face.

The train was quiet. It was very crowded, mainly with discharged military men. Everyone was a stranger and all were obviously exhausted, so there was almost no loud talking. The only sound was that of the train wheels, echoing monotonously. The commander fell asleep. I felt hungry and remembered the box lunch of rice balls I had been given when I left Omura, but it seemed like too much trouble to take them out. I dozed off, then fell into a deep sleep and slept for quite a long time.

I had wanted to see Hiroshima, but we were already long past the city when I opened my eyes again. I asked the soldier standing in the aisle next to me where we were. Okayama was far behind us and we would soon be coming to Himeji, he said. I looked at my watch and saw that it was four in the morning. I do not know whether the commander beside me had awakened in the meantime or not, but now he was as sound asleep as ever. I too was lulled to sleep again, and the next time I opened my eyes we were beyond Osaka. This time the commander was also awake.

By now the sun was fairly high in the sky. We said good morning to one another and fell into a conversation. Just then a totally unexpected event occurred. A soldier passing through the densely packed aisle in search of a place to stand was thrown off balance by the lurching of the train and started to fall on top of me. As he tried to maintain his footing, he stepped right on my baggage containing the specimen bottles. He was wearing sturdy army-supply boots, and whether he had actually broken one of the bottles or only cracked it, formaldehyde started to seep onto the floor. Its characteristic smell wafted through the car. Even the commander who knew what was in my baggage commented, "What a strong smell. My eyes are stinging."

If his surprise was great, the surprise and annoyance of the ex-servicemen, who had no idea what the smell was, were immensely greater. "What a strange smell." "Who brought that strange stuff on board?" "Call the conductor!" The commotion grew. Reluctantly I stood up and with some embarrassment began to explain the situation. "That smell is formaldehyde, which is used to preserve anatomical specimens. One of the bottles seems to have broken. I am sorry to have upset you, but it is not at all poisonous, and fortunately the windows are open so the smell will soon go away. Please try to put up with it just a little while longer."

It was not a very persuasive explanation, and after my rather lame apology, the commotion only grew louder. "How stupid to bring that sort of thing onto a crowded train." "Throw his stuff out the window!" Already hot and tired and hungry, the soldiers were further upset because the train had come to a standstill and was not moving an inch. I became the object of all their pent-up frustrations. And probably there was the additional element of the antagonism felt by enlisted men toward officers because of the special treatment given us during the war.

It was all too clear what would happen if mass psychology formed these frustrated soldiers into a mob. Already someone had said, "Throw his stuff out the window." No doubt they would join forces and toss my precious specimens out onto the tracks. If I put my hands together and pleaded with them, the pitiful sight would only drive them to feel greater triumph at their success. That my personal efforts should come to nothing was not important. What was irreparable was the loss of these medical specimens that testified to the horrors of acute radiation, and that the voices and prayers of the dead should fade without a trace and be lost in oblivion.

"Throw them out, right now." "I can't stand the smell." "I can't take it any longer." Confronted with the abnormal excitement of these high-strung soldiers, I could only cower nervously. But just then the commander next to me stood up and roared, "Shut up!" His well-trained voice reverberated amidst the uproar. "What do you think is preserved in that formaldehyde? The guts of the people who died in the special bombing at Nagasaki, that's what. This doctor is continuing his research in order to pray for the repose of those victims. The smell will soon go away, so just put up with it until it does." Whether it was his authoritative tone that was effective or they were moved by mention of the bomb victims, I do not know, but the train grew suddenly quiet and the commotion stopped.

I expressed my deep gratitude to the commander who rescued me and asked for his name and address. He smiled but did not answer. "I am going as far as

Shizuoka" was all he would say. The train arrived at
Nagoya. In order to get to Karuizawa, I had to
transfer to a train heading for Nagano. Fortunately
many people were getting off at Nagoya, and the stop
there was quite long. I thanked the commander again,
said goodbye, and started to unload my baggage.
There was no way that I could carry off in one load the
baggage that both Iyonaga and I had carried on. Just
then, however, someone silently lent a helping hand.
When I turned to see who it was, I felt sure he was
one of those who had demanded that I "throw the
stinking stuff out." A warm feeling flooded my heart.

I have totally forgotten what happened from the
time I changed trains at Nagoya until I finally arrived
in Karuizawa. The connections were bad in those
days, but I have not the faintest idea now where I
changed trains or how I managed with my baggage.
But I do remember what happened after I arrived at
Karuizawa Station. In front of the station was the
porter who, as always, called me "Sonny," in spite of
my lieutenant's stripes. With his help, I arrived home
with my baggage just after my mother and sister had
finished lunch.

Thinking back on it, from the time I left the gates of
Omura Naval Hospital, I had traveled two whole days
and nights with those specimens. But our journey together was not yet over. I only spent two nights at
home, then I repacked the specimens, loaded them on
my shoulders, and set off for Sendai. The formaldehyde that had leaked out on the train had come
from one small glass jar containing a fragment of brain

tissue. None of the other containers showed any signs of damage.

It had been a long time since I had been to Sendai, and the city, devastated by air raids, had changed beyond recognition. But my alma mater was still functioning, and I was able to see many of my former professors. I divided the precious specimens that I had carried all the way from Nagasaki between the departments of pathology and surgery at the Tohoku University Faculty of Medicine, with the prayer that these medical data might prove useful for the peace of the human race.

At that moment, at last, the war had come to an end for me.

Pursuing the Study of Man

Though still antipathetic to doctors, after the war I continued to practice medicine. I had become a navy doctor whether I had wanted to or not because of the special circumstance of war. But basically I had entered medicine as one way to study man himself.

My attitudes toward medicine remained the same after the war. I had only a basic grounding in medicine when I found myself tending the victims of the atomic bomb. That extreme experience provoked in me a desire to learn more about psychiatry, and so I entered the psychiatry department of the University of Tokyo School of Medicine and began to pursue psychiatry as a humanistic discipline under Professor Sukeyuki Uchimura.

The specimens that I had left behind at Omura Naval Hospital preyed on my mind, but now that I had no affiliations there, I was unlikely to receive permission to go back and get them. More than a month had passed since I had been demobilized, and the con-

trol of Omura Naval Hospital had been transferred
to Nagasaki Medical College (the precursor of today's
Nagasaki University School of Medicine), and thus the
place had become increasingly removed from me. All
that I could do was pray that the organs of those victims might prove useful for the study of radiation
sickness and for the peace of mankind.

I did visit the old Omura Naval Hospital once again
seven years later. Although I was not a specialist in the
field, I had published a report on the care of the atomic
bomb victims and on the findings of their autopsies. As
a result, I had been asked by the faculty board of the
Nagasaki University Medical School and the Nagasaki
Medical Association to deliver a lecture there. On the
way to Nagasaki, I stopped in at Omura Hospital.
Since my time, it had become a national hospital with
a totally different administration. The "depository"
where Iyonaga and I had stored the pathology specimens was now completely different. No matter where
I looked, I could find no trace of those specimens.
Control of the hospital had been shifted first from the
navy to Nagasaki Medical College and from there
to the national hospital system, and after these two
changes in administration, no one now had any idea
what had happened to the specimens.

According to records made when the control of
Omura Naval Hospital was transferred to Nagasaki
Medical College, the new director of the hospital was
Professor Raisuke Shirabe of the surgery department;
Professor Takeuchi and Associate Professor Wakahara
were in charge of pathology; and Associate Professor

Sato was in charge of anatomy. I tried to follow these leads but found no one who knew anything about the pathology specimens of the atomic bomb victims. After I left, the remaining specimens may have once again been thrown out and left to their fate on the mountain. I could only imagine that the worst had happened to them, and I left Omura this time with a dismal feeling.

For some reason, I could not help remembering what it had been like when I left Omura seven years before: the looks of those patients who were totally dependent on me, unable even to complain of their agony; that girl's clear, quiet eyes; the young girls of the Women's Volunteer Corps, who, though fully aware of their own approaching death, devotedly continued to nurse others; the many people who even now are passing each day in suffering. I stifled the memories in my heart and left Omura, resolved anew to pursue psychiatry as a way of studying humanity.

THE ATOMIC BOMB EXPERIENCE: SELECTED ESSAYS

PART TWO

THE ATOMIC BOMB EXPERIENCE:
SELECTED ESSAYS

Introduction:
The Enigmatic Slip of Paper

In October 1945, I entered the psychiatry department of the University of Tokyo and began my studies in this new field. Almost every day and night of my student life was spent in the laboratory. I slept there and even cooked my meals on a portable stove I had brought in with me. It was a time when all daily essentials, especially food, were practically nonexistent, and the atmosphere was hardly conducive to complete devotion to scholarship.

Nevertheless, compared to the events at Omura two months earlier, it seemed all too peaceful, all too serene. A clear blue October sky floated over the vast burned-out wasteland that Tokyo had become, and I felt a strange lightheartedness accompanied by a sense of lethargy. "Perhaps now I can finally lead a normal life!"—such buoyant expectations would often elate me, but in the next moment I would inevitably recall the faces and appearance of the Nagasaki atomic bomb victims. From that time to this very day, though the road I have taken has led from psychiatry to neurosurgery, I have never at any time been free of my fateful connection with the atomic bomb. Perhaps I might even say that the atomic bomb experience itself has been my own personal postwar history.

Shortly after the end of the war, for example, a faculty association was organized at the University of Tokyo, and I was often asked to speak about the bombing of Nagasaki at their meetings. I seem to have been the only member of the faculty association—in those days, at any rate—to have witnessed with my own eyes the horrors of the atomic bomb. But when I came to relate in detail the destruction the bomb had wrought, a small slip of paper was passed to me by one of the association members. On it was written, "Please be careful what you say. There is a detective here from the Motofuji police station."

At first I could not imagine what was going on. In the first place, wasn't Japan the *victim* of the atomic bomb? There could be no possible reason for anyone to get into trouble for telling the truth. How could something like this happen, I wondered. Not until much later did I realize that it was a policy of the U.S. occupation forces to restrict discussion of the atomic bomb. But such a reaction has not been confined only to the Americans. I have been confronted countless times by attitudes to the bomb held by Japanese and other peoples of the world which I find incomprehensible and infuriating. It has at times driven me to deep despair; it has also forced me to speak out, often in a voice of agonized impatience.

What I have published in newspapers and magazines I have kept in ready access and would like to include here in chronological order and with almost no changes to the original texts. I know that these essays convey the exasperation and powerlessness that an eyewitness of the atomic bombing of Nagasaki feels toward everyone who has not experienced the event. And yet I hope that they suggest a more universal message as well.

I Can No Longer Keep Silent

Kaizo (Reconstruction)
1952

The other day while leafing through a popular U.S. magazine, I came across a picture of a patient lying on a bed under clean white sheets being injected with some sort of fluid while a doctor and nurse in spotless uniforms stood by. The accompanying text was headlined: "Medical Attention Given to Victims of the Atom Bomb," and it contained an account of the different types of medical care available to bomb victims at the finest medical facilities. The first thought that entered my head when I saw this article was, "What kind of impractical, theoretical nonsense is this?" And I was unable to repress the urge to cry out at the ignorance and utter foolishness of such a view of treatment for victims of the atomic bomb.

Relief by such impractical fantasies described in the magazine article might be worth contemplating if there were even a remote chance such help were possible. But what would it mean if an atomic bomb were to explode in the air above a city? All physical objects in the city would be blown to bits or destroyed by fire, and almost all its citizens would writhe in agony from injuries or burns and be exposed to radioactivity. The streets would be filled with the pathetic sight of people crawling in search of water and those of the wounded still able to move carrying the more critically injured on boards, trying to flee as far as possible from the scene. We cannot imagine that the fate of doctors and hospital workers—not to mention hospital facilities— would be any different from that which had befallen the rest of the city. The experiences of Hiroshima and Nagasaki make this fact all too clear.

Where in such a devastated city could one find a bed with such a soft downy mattress, such a healthy doctor ready and able to work, such a kindhearted and beautiful nurse? Where would medicine, bandages, or even a single sterilized needle be left preserved in good condition? It is as clear as daylight that to reduplicate the treatment depicted in that magazine photograph all the medical equipment, doctors, and nurses from several surrounding towns would have to be mobilized and the injured transported there by all possible means; even then, such idealized treatment could be given only to a very small fraction of the bomb victims.

I was told that at a suburban hospital to which were admitted those victims who had with difficulty been rescued from Hiroshima, the medical personnel walked their feet off night and day simply in order to give a single drink of water to each patient who asked for it. They could give no medical treatment there at

all. The utmost they were able to accomplish was to
give the dying one last sip of water.

I have direct experience caring for atomic bomb victims, and I feel compelled to bear witness to the horrible reality of what it was like. When the atomic bomb
fell on Nagasaki, I was stationed at a suburban naval
hospital that had escaped direct damage from the
blast. Around eleven o'clock in the morning, the un-
forgettable flash of light from the bomb seared itself
onto my retina. By twelve that night, 758 victims, a
mere fraction of the total number of casualties, were
brought to us in conditions pitiful beyond words.

This hospital was equipped with material provisions
and personnel to care for some two thousand patients.
Such facilities not withstanding, what were we actually
able to do for these 758 people? Our huge organization, with the finest facilities and an incomparable
staff, worked late into the following morning, and yet
all we could do was give these patients extremely ordinary—and inadequate—treatment for general burns
and injuries.

Having lain first in the fire-swept streets of Nagasaki, then in transport trains, and finally trucks onto
which they had been loaded like cattle, the victims
finally arrived at the hospital twelve hours after they
had first been injured and in such weakened condition that very few had even the strength to ask for a
glass of water. Many of them were nothing more than
charred and blackened lumps of flesh waiting for im-
pending death.

When I applied my stethoscope to one patient who

complained of chest pains, I heard a rattling sound every time he breathed. After giving him a few words of encouragement, I had an X-ray taken and discovered that some of the fragments of glass piercing the whole surface of his body had penetrated into his lungs. Could even the finest chest surgeon today have relieved this deadly condition? And this is merely one example of the external injuries these bomb victims had sustained. When such wounds were accompanied by burns and radiation poisoning, even if the most famous physicians from all over the country had been gathered together in one room, what could they possibly have done? If this was the state of affairs for patients fortunate enough to be carried away from the scene of the bombing to a very well-equipped hospital, what the doctors at the scene would be able to do is hardly worth considering.

Even if, for the time being, we suppose that the effects of the atomic bomb were limited to external injuries, it produces so many casualties that caring for these victims alone would soon be beyond human capacities. When these external injuries are accompanied by burns and particularly by radiation sickness, which cannot be cured despite all the efforts of present-day medical science, it is clear that all we can do is throw up our hands and declare the situation hopeless.

No one except the victims who managed to survive Hiroshima and Nagasaki and those who had to deal with them knows the truth about the new weapon called the atomic bomb—that it produces horrifying and uncontrollable damage unlike anything ever known. It is only natural that everyone else is unaware of this. That is all the more reason for those of us who do know the truth to speak out. We must teach what we know to others. This is our absolute duty.

And yet some say that now is not the time to make this truth known. Why not? "Because it runs contrary to the wishes of those in power. We should stick to our research," they say. Such a complacent attitude on the part of scholars who pride themselves on their learning is not confined only to the atomic bomb issue. This kind of cowardly reasoning, I must say, is the same indulged in by opportunist politicians.

It is certainly a great achievement and a gratifying development that science, whose aim is the systematization of truth, has succeeded in tapping nuclear energy. Setting aside the pros and cons of the use of this wonderful energy source in the atomic bomb, the bomb's success is clearly the fruit of scientific effort. But it is the fundamental duty of scientists today to convey to nonspecialists that the fruits of this success which the scientific community has achieved are in fact very bitter, a terrible misfortune for the entire world.

The Conference that Never Convened

Kaizo
1952

As I am sure each and every one of my readers is well aware from the articles appearing in all the October fifteenth newspapers, the International Conference of Medical Practitioners, which was to hear the world's first comprehensive report about atomic bomb injuries, was suddenly suppressed by the Italian government just before it was to open in Monte Catini.

This news has caused quite a shock not only to us specialists in the field who have had to overcome repeated obstacles and repression to get this far, but even to the general public who are interested in and concerned about the atomic bomb. Poignant pleas for the convening of this conference as soon as possible have been heard from all quarters in letters to all the newspapers throughout the country and in every other forum of public opinion.

On the other hand, there certainly seem to be many people who suspect that the conference was a part of the program of the so-called "peace offensive," or one phase of a movement instigated by political motives of some kind. For people with such suspicions, the suppression of the conference is probably dismissed as altogether right and proper. Meanwhile, there is a group with quite the opposite philosophy, which tries to exploit not only the suppression of this conference but any and every similar incident for its party's political purposes. It is not hard to imagine that for them the present situation must be extremely useful, since it has become the focus of attention for Japanese from all walks of life and the forces moving behind the Italian government's decision can so easily be inferred.

Against this complex background, I would like to consider the future of this medical conference, which was organized by well-intentioned scholars from all over the world, motivated purely by their consciences as scientists. I hope that what I say may serve as an aid to a better understanding of what the physicians of the world had in mind and what we were hoping to do there.

WHAT IS THE INTERNATIONAL CONFERENCE OF MEDICAL PRACTITIONERS?

Since the end of the war, we have heard more and more often about this international meeting or that world conference, so that we may be tempted to call the present day the Age of the International Conference. The newspapers are filled with photographs of scholars leaving, bouquet in hand, from Haneda or

Yokohama for such conferences or with articles about their elaborate sendoffs. By contrast, however, almost no information is given about what these people did at their conferences, what sort of things were agreed upon, when our representatives came back to Japan, or what reports they made upon their return. Occasionally a few lines about so-and-so's return home can be found at the bottom of some back page, but that is about all. And that is generally to inform us that part of the public's money has been converted into such souvenirs from abroad as the latest fashions and gold watches, which there are quite enough of here already.

What expectations about international conferences can Japanese possibly hold when they know they are nothing but publicly financed foreign vacations? To be honest, I myself have been one of these pessimists. But toward the end of last summer, I received an appeal to attend a meeting about the newly formed International Conference of Medical Practitioners. My first reaction can be summed up as "not another one!" and I had a very negative attitude to the whole idea. But as a token of respect to several of my distinguished senior colleagues who went out of their way to urge me to join, I went to a meeting held to explain something about the organization.

I sat there at this small gathering of people, knowing neither the objectives of the International Conference of Medical Practitioners nor even where it was based, but before the program had even begun, the first thing I noticed was that some of the foremost scientists in Japan were present. My first impression was that with these people behind it, the conference could accomplish something. As we moved rapidly through the agenda, I even forgot about the conference itself, so thrilled was I at hearing the speeches of these wise and learned men. Then the following account was given of how the proposed conference had first originated.

In April 1951, a meeting of delegates from France, Italy, and several other European countries was held in Naples to deal with national health problems. At that time the dynamic proposal was made at the urging of Dr. Bourguignon, professor of physiology at Paris University, that specialists from all over the world gather together to discuss these issues. With Dr. Bourguignon as the driving force behind the plan, invitations were immediately sent to all the countries of Europe, and a preparatory committee was set up in Paris. After a discussion of various topics the committee concluded that the present international climate produced by the division of the world into two opposing camps constitutes a threat to world peace and that, as a result, even cultural exchange cannot be sufficiently and satisfactorily carried on. In the light of this situation and from the perspective of what the world's doctors could do to alleviate it, the committee affirmed the need to grapple with three problems: (1) medical progress and the preservation of peace; (2) the effects of war on a nation's health; and (3) the damage done to medical progress by the interruption of cross-cultural cooperation. To further these aims it was decided to avoid influence from governments or the subtle workings of international politics by eliciting directly the opinions of interested medical scientists and practitioners. Announcements were sent personally to prominent physicians in every country of the world.

In the medical sciences, there are numerous gatherings of the same ilk as the international conferences held in other fields. These conferences are sponsored by administrative systems like WHO (the World Health Organization) or are specialized meetings of some branch of medicine like surgery or dentistry. Furthermore, most of these tend to be nothing more than occasions for sociable merrymaking and end up having produced very little if anything of value. In light of this state of affairs, the plans for this conference were quite significant, for it promised to be an opportunity to return medicine to its true nature as the study of the weak and the sick of this world and a place to discuss issues freely without regard to which side of the Iron Curtain one was on.

In Japan, announcements of the proposed conference were sent to professors Hisomu Nagai and Kiyoshi Shiga and, surely by some mistake, to me as well, though I am still a mere novice, serving my apprenticeship in the university psychiatry laboratory. The three of us who received these letters and others concerned then had to decide what stand we should take as Japanese medical practitioners interested in these problems.

Many opinions were exchanged, but no conclusions were reached because, in addition to lack of sufficient information about the conference, there was the fear lest it turn out to be a political meeting hiding behind the word peace. But taking into consideration the fact that it had been proposed by no less a personage than Dr. Bourguignon, the president of the French Academy and a man of considerable reputation in academic circles, we decided to view the conference as a cross-cultural medical movement and to send a reply stating our intention to form our own preparatory committee in Japan. Forthwith we put professors Shiga and Nagai in charge of the Japanese preparatory committee and appointed as our director Dr. Takashi Hayashi, professor of physiology at the Faculty of Medicine of Keio University.

We immediately sent notices to the medical schools of all the universities and to every level of the Japanese medical world, and on September 15, 1951, the Japanese preparatory committee of the International Conference of Medical Practitioners met at Kitazato Memorial Hall in Keio Hospital. In spite of some defamatory remarks from one quarter of the medical world about the purposes of the conference, more than two hundred distinguished professors and physicians attended the meeting that day, including Hiroshige Shioda, head of the medical sciences division of the Japan Science Council.

There was a heated discussion among the various specialists about what agenda to send to conference headquarters from Japan, but it was finally decided that, though we could not send representatives because of the expenses involved and for other reasons, we could contribute data on the following four topics: (1) our experiences with and views about the atomic bomb; (2) the establishment of facilities for the international exchange of medical information; (3) the question of social security; and (4) exchange of data on public health. In addition to this report, we appended a postscript to the effect that if, in the future, the organization were to come under political pressures or influence, it would be difficult for us Japanese medical practitioners to continue our cooperation. Then we sent off our reply to conference headquarters in Paris.

Various committees were formed in Japan to deal with each of the four topics we had proposed, and at the same time appeals for support were being made to the whole country with greater and greater vigor. Meanwhile, in Europe, meetings of the preparatory committee were held several times preliminary to the main conference to discuss the data assembled from the participating countries. Once Italy had been decided on as the conference host, preparations began in earnest in Rome under the direction of Dr. Massenti, a professor of Rome University Medical School. The formal name for the conference was no longer simply the International Conference of Medical Practitioners but the World Medical Conference for Research into Existing Living Conditions.

The news about the report on atomic bomb injuries in the agenda sent by Japan evoked the greatest reaction among the participants. A request for all available information on the subject was received not long afterwards. Upon receipt of this request, the Japanese preparatory committee decided, for financial reasons among others, to focus all its energies on the atomic bomb issue and to provide the conference all possible assistance. At the same time, appeals for the participation of Japanese representatives to the conference were gradually growing stronger, and after repeated meetings, mainly of the secretariat, the names of three representatives were formally decided upon and sent to Rome.

In July, the conference's official program was sent to us. As soon as we saw it, those of us in the secretariat concerned with the atomic bomb issue felt more than ever the heavy burden of our responsibility, for almost the entire final day of the three-day conference had been reserved for the representatives from Japan.

From then on the members of the secretariat grew so busy that we had to put aside our regular work to keep up with communications with conference headquarters. At the same time, we were busily engaged in organizing the report data and making the travel preparations for our delegation. The costs of the delegation were covered by contributions from medical circles and from the general public. During this period, the Italian government and authorities in the Japanese Ministry of Foreign Affairs were helpful in making travel arrangements and in other affairs of an international nature and, in general, well-disposed to us far beyond our expectations.

ASSEMBLING DATA ON ATOMIC BOMB INJURIES

On September 15, 1951, at the meeting at which we Japanese doctors declared our intention to participate in the International Conference of Medical Practitioners, various items for the agenda were proposed, and it was only natural that the report on atomic bomb injuries should occupy the most central place among them. There were even some who insisted that we should depart from our position as doctors and issue a ban-the-bomb statement. The majority opposed this suggestion, however, and it was decided to stick to a medical account of the issue.

As mentioned earlier, a committee was immediately formed to collect data and soon set to work, but from the beginning it ran into obstacles and difficulties that had never been anticipated. The first reason for these difficulties was that there was strikingly little medical data about atomic bomb casualties available in print. Not only photographs of bomb victims but even medical research findings were considered unpublishable during the occupation. In fact, some material was actually suppressed by the authorities.

Take for example, the case of Dr. Masao Tsuzuki (1895–1961), professor of surgery at the University of Tokyo. Dr. Tsuzuki had been a navy doctor with the rank of rear admiral and so had automatically been purged when the war ended. He was later cleared in a special communication from GHQ and ordered to work as the Japanese head of an inquiry into the damage caused by the atomic bomb. However, as soon as he had with great effort assembled a portion of his findings and distributed one hundred copies to those immediately involved, he was once again sentenced to be purged. This harsh treatment, however, was not given to the authors of several other articles on the same subject which were published in ordinary scientific journals. Even occupation policy did not take the extreme step of completely suppressing all publication of reports of atomic bomb damage.

But the psychological effect of this instance of suppression had great repercussions, and everyone decided it was safer for the time being to file away their precious data and not attempt to publish anything. Thus it was that in August 1951, just when the question of whether to participate in the International Conference of Medical Practitioners was being raised throughout the country, summaries of the report on the investigation into atomic bomb damage (*Genshi Bakudan Saigai Chosa Shiryo Hokokusho*) were published by the Japanese Council for the Promotion of Science, and a printed work on the subject of the atomic bomb became publicly available for the first time since the war.

Using the names of the researchers mentioned in this report and their articles as our only lead, we set to work. In the meantime, we searched for the many other researchers whose works had not been included in the report and made appeals for help to every other possible source. It was at this point, however, that our second obstacle lay in wait for us. We discovered that an extremely large number of people were still afraid to publish their research findings, partly because they feared criticism from certain sectors within the medical world.

Perhaps this was a sign of the closed nature of Japanese medical circles, but at any rate the tendency to avoid personal responsibility had grown stronger. Someone even made the explicitly political pronouncement that "as doctors we are well aware of the seriousness of the damage, but we do not consider it a proper scientific attitude to make this knowledge public under these circumstances." I took a different tack by arguing that this was the best opportunity to make the facts known to the world's medical circles on both sides of the Iron Curtain and that now was the time for the Japanese medical world to make its stand.

No matter how you look at it, though, it is difficult to understand why nothing was ever printed of the findings assembled through the efforts of Professor Shun'ichi Mashimo of Kyoto University and numerous others like him who faced dangers of all kinds right after the bombing while pursuing their research.

Though beset with many difficulties, our work proceeded steadily. This was thanks to the efforts of Professor Hitoshi Miyake of the University of Tokyo Pathology Department, who was an active member of the Science Council's research committee; Associate Professor Nakao of internal medicine; Dr. Shiraki of psychiatry; and many, many others. Special mention must be made here too of the active assistance and general guidance we received from Dr. Tsuzuki.

The articles we were finally able to gather together

numbered in excess of 240. Some of the participants even took field trips to Hiroshima and Nagasaki to make follow-up reports on their original research. The Nagasaki Medical College, in particular, along with the prefectural and city medical associations, enthusiastically helped us, and many specialists under Professor Raisuke Shirabe of surgery lent us large quantities of data.

Our next problem was how to organize and make readily intelligible all the data we had managed to assemble. After considering many proposals, we finally decided on the following methods. First, to exhibit at the conference hall over two hundred photographs of the general destruction which the atomic bomb caused both to buildings and the physical environment, and also to present the specifically medical damage as revealed in clinical and microscopic examinations. The photographs were donated not only by those in the medical profession but by a broad spectrum of people from all walks of life.

Our second method had to do with means of communication. We could not hope to give an adequate exposition of the problems in the limited time allowed for us to speak. Taking into consideration as well our linguistic handicaps, we decided to make up a pamphlet to be distributed to all the delegates. Our intention was to make a pamphlet to cover the material the three Japanese representatives would be presenting in their speeches. This would give both detailed scientific information and yet convey to the reader a general sense of the nature of atomic bomb damage. Our fifty-page Japanese manuscript plus charts and photographs was then translated into English. Next, a draft of what ideas and assertions our three representatives should present in their oral statements was drawn up on the basis of what was contained in the pamphlet. The gist of their statements can be summarized by the following three points: (1) even with all of our technical expertise, medical science cannot cure the effects of radiation exposure; (2) the atomic bomb produces an enormous number of casualties in a single instant; and (3) unlike injuries produced in ordinary bombings, uneasiness about future physical aftereffects still remains. What we particularly wanted to emphasize was that modern medical science is next to powerless in the face of the atomic bomb.

THE ITALIAN GOVERNMENT'S SUPPRESSION OF THE CONFERENCE

With the scheduled opening of the conference on October 16, 1952 near at hand, the preparations for sending our representatives were proceeding smoothly. Then, suddenly, on September 16, we received a telegram from conference headquarters in Rome which read: "Conference may be slightly delayed. Please await further instructions." At the time, we thought that probably some technical formalities on the part of the various participating countries remained to be completed, but not long afterwards we received the following message from the chairman of the conference, Professor Massenti: "Due to circumstances beyond our control, it has now become imperative that you send us immediately the entire contents of the report the Japanese delegation intends to present.''

With no means at our disposal to find out the truth of the matter, we had no choice but to send to Rome the contents of the talks our three delegates planned to give. We did so, and by return mail we received a message which caused us extreme apprehension: ''For the continuance of this conference, it is important that the Japanese delegation absolutely refrain from raising political issues.''

Without knowing what had happened within the conference host country of Italy, we were forced to call off the departure of our delegation and wait further word. And then a message was delivered to the Japanese Foreign Ministry through the Italian Embassy. When we heard it, we could scarcely believe our ears. ''Please inform the parties concerned that the International Conference of Medical Practitioners to be held in Monte Catini has been canceled. We trust that absolute discretion will be shown. The Italian Embassy will appreciate the Japanese Foreign Ministry's judicious handling of this matter.''

The contents of the message were extremely vague, but for the first time the intervention of the Italian government in this matter came to light. The Japan secretariat, having been assured by telegram from conference headquarters that we would be informed immediately of any new developments, waited for a formal announcement. On October 7, the official document arrived.

According to this letter, the Italian government, which had given its full cooperation during the past year, suddenly on September 15 prohibited the conference from opening. In spite of repeated negotiations, no clear explanation of the reasons for this action had yet been given. After several meetings of the European executive committees, it had been decided to abandon plans to convene the conference in Italy. Instead, preparations had begun to hold a conference with exactly the same agenda in a Scandinavian country sometime before the middle of April next year. Scientists from all over the world had sent letters to the Italian government protesting its action as an alarming infringement of academic freedom and the fundamental rights of scientists.

From the facts I have just related, I think it is fairly clear why the International Conference of Medical Practitioners had been canceled. Considering the fact that for more than a year, during which preparations for the conference were being made there, the Italian government never once showed any signs of opposition, but suddenly, without providing any reasons, banned the conference just before it was about to begin, it seems quite reasonable for the conference organizers to interpret these actions as due to political forces "beyond our control." Likewise, it is clear that the reason for the cancellation had something to do with the message we received—that it had "become imperative that you send us immediately the entire contents of the report the Japanese delegation intends to present." In other words, the decision was somehow related to our report on atomic bomb injuries.

There was no conceivable reason for the Italian government to be averse to a report on injuries caused by the atomic bomb. And even if there had been, they would have adopted some countermeasures much earlier, when they first learned of the report. They would not have waited until the last minute to cancel the conference without even an explanation for their actions.

If not the Italian government, then what political power was averse to this report? And did that power intervene with the government of Italy? In this age, governments avoid making blatant moves that any ordinary person can see through. It would be a blunder to say that other issues may be discussed at such a conference, but not the atomic bomb. That would make the motive for the cancellation, and its agents, all too clear. There are any number of convenient, plausible reasons for cancellation that can be exploited without making a public issue out of the atomic bomb. In other words, it was easier to confuse the issue by suppressing the conference entirely.

It is not necessary to investigate this affair any further. There are, after all, no secrets that remain secret for all time. Particularly in a case like this, where repeated negotiations have been carried on, it is inevitable that little by little, here and there, the truth will come to light. And when all these fragmentary revelations are put together a uniform pattern will emerge.

Does any European nation have the power to bring to bear this amount of pressure on the Italian government? On the other hand, the Soviet bloc, judging from its usual political stance and past record, would have reason to welcome, not oppose, a report on the atomic bomb. In fact, it would probably like to get its hands on our report as soon as possible and publish our data, making it known throughout the world— for its own purposes, of course. The Soviet eagerness to exploit the nuclear issue for propaganda purposes is particularly distressing to the Western European camp. It was precisely our anxiety about the state of confrontation between the two camps that made the Japan secretariat deliberate the matter with all due caution and decide to participate in the conference only on the condition that we could present our findings impartially to both sides of the Iron Curtain at the same time.

And thus we discovered that what we feared might happen had, in fact, occurred. I do not know the precise details, but judging from the decision of international headquarters to make the next site for the conference a Scandinavian country, thus steering clear of the NATO bloc entirely, the most justifiable conclusion is that that political power which has the greatest influence over Western Europe was actively at work behind the scenes in Italy.

Be that as it may, the fact that a country which boasts of freedom has suppressed a scientific conference is a severe blow to the hopes of humanity. Apart from medical conferences with a clear political leaning, like the recent problematic Peking conference, this is the first medical conference in history to have been suppressed by political force. What is important now is not to remain passive simply because it is difficult to bring to light the true facts or simply because the shadow of a certain political power is clearly visible in the background. I was roundly scolded when I expressed the opinion at a meeting of the Japan secretariat that it should not matter that some people consider the conference tinged with political bias, as long as we convey our findings impartially to all sides under circumstances where all other conditions are favorable and everyone is acting according to his own free will. I sincerely believe that having an accurate account of the damage wrought by the atomic bomb disseminated as soon as possible to the four corners of the world is the most pressing problem in this troubled world of ours. And so at this meeting the Japan secretariat began preparations to send to the secretariats of all the other participating countries the pamphlets we had planned to distribute at the conference.

I have recorded here some of my personal inferences and surmises about the suppression of the conference, but I realize that an action like the protest recently made against the Italian government is only a formality. The authorities who were forced by circumstances into this painful position are truly to be pitied. Nor do I assign too much significance to the protest itself. What is important now are our efforts to make known to as many people as possible by any means possible, even personal letters, the truth about the damage caused by the atomic bomb.

Medical Science
and the Atomic Bomb

Kahoku Shimpo (Kahoku News)
May 8, 1953

Recently I came across the term "atomic bomb medicine" (*gembaku igaku*). At first glance, this collocation of words sounds quite all right and even seems to make a sort of sense. But if you think about it a bit longer, it really is a strange expression. Just what in fact is atomic bomb medicine? Phrases such as this one which end in the word *igaku* (medicine or medical science) are often used in Japanese. Everyday in the newspapers we find references to the advanced state of *kekkaku igaku* (tuberculosis medicine) or to *seishin igaku* (psychiatry). At one time there was even talk of *senso igaku* (war medicine). What all these terms refer to are the specialized branches of medicine which treat the conditions described by the first word in each phrase. In that case, "atomic bomb medicine" would mean the branch of medical science which specializes in treating injuries caused by the atomic bomb.

What we must now consider is the meaning of the academic discipline known as medical science. If we were to divide medical science into broad areas, there would be, first of all, studies into what constitutes the state of health and the state of disease, and, next, research into how to cure disease. Specialists in tuberculosis, for example, investigate the ontology of the disease and, once its causes are understood, try to eradicate them. Psychiatry is the study of the sound state of mental health and the disturbed or unbalanced state and the attempt to restore normality.

It would be a contradiction, of course, to speak of "homicidal medicine" (*hitogoroshi igaku*), though people use with surprising casualness an extremely similar expression when they speak of war medicine. This latter phrase, too, refers to the contradictory aim of restoring to some sort of health the wounded body of a victim of man's murderous inhumanity to man.

If we think of it in this way, atomic bomb medicine, like homicidal medicine, is a totally meaningless term. Medical science based on evildoing is inconceivable. And yet, we cannot let suffering go unattended just because its causes are evil. Such a proposition, taken to its logical conclusion, would result in the neglect of most clinical objects of medical science. The goal of medical science is to eliminate the patient's suffering and try to alleviate his condition no matter what may have caused it.

But has any doctor anywhere in the world come up with a complete medical cure for the injuries caused by the atomic bomb? The best we in the medical profession can do is to make it common knowledge that medicine is helpless against the injuries the bomb causes and to take a firm stand against its use so that this tragic cause of suffering never occurs again. At present no medical scientist is studying what to do when the atomic bomb falls. Anyone pursuing such research would have to be a madman or a charlatan exploiting the name of medicine.

Today, almost eight years after the war has ended, what have we learned about the atomic bomb from the research of scientists in the United States and Japan? We know, first of all, that the large majority of those in the bombed area die either the instant the bomb falls or soon afterwards. Second, most of the victims who seem likely to survive develop an incurable blood disorder and die within a few days or weeks. Third, even those who escape an immediate death are afflicted by keloid scars and other physical disabilities. Fourth, just as the cities of Hiroshima and Nagasaki were reduced to burned-out rubble, the internal organs of the dead are subjected to appalling devastation. And finally, more time is needed before any conclusions can yet be made about the ultimate fate of the surviving victims.

Medical science has been making steady progress, and yet it has its hands full simply studying diseases with natural causes. It can ill afford to pursue the study of man-made suffering as well. If medical science and the atomic bomb must be linked together at all, it should only be in a preventive medicine whose object is the pathological psychological condition of those people who have abused the causes of science by employing atomic energy in such an evil way.

Atomic Bomb Disease

Shizen (Nature)
May 1952

THE CRUELTY OF ATOMIC BOMB DISEASE

Nowadays photographs of the human devastation wrought by the atomic bomb are seen everywhere—the charred faces, the ugly keloid scars left by burns, the backs embedded all over with glass fragments, the blackened corpses like lumps of charcoal.

Such sights have been indelibly imprinted on people's minds, overwhelming many with an indescribable feeling of horror and revulsion. Different people have received different impressions, of course, but I imagine that the most vivid is "I don't want to see this ever again." That reaction is only natural, I believe; in fact, it is what any respectable person should feel. For that very reason, this sort of photograph exhibition will always produce the same results. At worst, it may even end up making people respond with the same bored cynicism as they do to the pictures of murder victims or of horrifying automobile

166

accidents often shown in American news magazines.

To put the matter another way, it is possible that photographs of atomic bomb casualties may, in fact, distract attention from the truth and prevent an accurate understanding of how terrible the destruction caused by the atomic bomb really was. The external injuries depicted in photographic documents of this kind are not representative of the extent of the damage, nor can photographs adequately convey the terrible dysfunctions produced deep within the body.

In general, people only know in theory that the tremendously powerful explosive known as the atomic bomb causes not only burns and other external injuries but produces some kind of special internal damage as well. They have no clear idea of what specific disorders occur or what problems these cause. In particular, it is not generally understood that medical science is close to powerless against the workings of the atomic bomb.

When someone hears the atomic bomb and medical science mentioned at the same time, he may get the impression that research is being done into some sort of treatment for atomic bomb induced injuries, and he is led to believe that, if worst comes to worst, everything will be all right as long as victims receive medical attention. But that, in fact, is not the case. At present, the problem under investigation by specialists is merely a scientific inquiry into just how awful this internal damage really is. In the face of such horrifying damage, it is impossible even to imagine any kind of medical treatment.

Taking these facts into consideration, I would like to review once again what sort of injuries were caused by the atomic bomb that fell on Hiroshima and Nagasaki. The major characteristic of the atomic bomb in action is that it produces at one time radioactivity, intense heat, and a powerful blast, all immeasurably greater than anything hitherto known.

First of all, the blast exerted enormous pressures of between five and ten tons per square meter directly below the point of explosion (in Nagasaki, this was about five hundred meters above the ground) or the equivalent of several two-ton trucks running into a human being at extremely high speed. The violent heat of the bomb is said to the same intensity as the sun if, in a single moment, it were to fall to a point several hundred meters above our heads. Supposing for the moment that there had been no radiation damage, it is easy to see that the blast and heat of the bomb alone are enough to kill a large majority of the people exposed, instantaneously or nearly so.

But in addition the bomb produced radiation sickness, which, even with all the resources at its disposal, modern medicine remains unable to cure. Radiation sickness, which begins to occur on the very day of the explosion, is accompanied by such symptoms as fever and bloody stools, as in the case of dysentery; by vomiting; and then by subcutaneous hemorrhaging and loss of hair. These phenomena occurred even in people who were fortunate enough to escape external injury at the time of the bombing, and one by one they all died within a few days.

This powerful radiation—colorless, odorless, entering the body without warning—invades and pervades all its parts, especially the blood-making apparatus, the reproductive system, the hair follicles, and other places which ceaselessly produce new cells. The organs of those who died from radiation poisoning received widespread and irreparable damage much like that sustained at the scenes of the bombing in Hiroshima and Nagasaki. If all the human organs whose function is to produce new life are destroyed, all that remains is inevitable and inexorable deterioration. A decrease in white blood corpuscles is particularly noticeable in victims of atomic radiation. As a result, the patient's body falls into a state of putrefaction, and nothing can be done but wait for him to die.

When seen under a microscope, this radiation-destroyed tissue conveys more eloquently than any photograph or verbal explanation of external injuries the indescribable horror of the atomic bomb. It is directly intelligible to the specialist as scientific proof with no further need of explanation. For those of us in the medical sciences, the wretched feeling inspired by the sight of this tissue is quite unlike anything we normally experience.

Such instances of atomic injuries would be more than enough all by themselves, but, in addition, extremely troublesome ailments have occurred among those who survived the first effects of the bomb. One such problem is keloids. Unlike scars left by ordinary burns, keloids (or cheloids) are loathsome fibrous growths which make ugly protrusions on the skin, as though the scars had flowed like molten lava or toffee. Patients with keloids are tormented day and night by itching and by stinging pain. Even when operated on, the scars remain as protuberant as ever and sometimes they even develop in the new surgical incisions.

What makes matters even worse is that modern medicine cannot fully explain the causes of keloids. Keloids have been known about for quite some time. They can occur with ordinary burns caused by scalding water or coal fires, and for some reason they can also be hereditary. Whether there is any direct connection between keloids and radiation is still unclear, and, in fact, the great majority of scientists deny any such relationship. Some specialists offer the explanation that keloids result from instantaneous exposure to extremely high temperatures, which causes the connective tissue directly under the skin to multiply abnormally. During the war, keloids similar to those found in atomic bomb victims were produced by high heat from incendiary bombs and gasoline explosions, for example.

In addition to keloids, leukemia, which is thought to be radiation-induced, has begun to appear among atomic bomb victims. This condition, just the reverse of the abnormal decline in white blood corpuscles which occurred in patients right after the bombing, is characterized by an excessive proliferation of white blood cells. An increase in the quantity of cells may seem like a good thing, but since these are all immature and ineffectual, on the contrary, they cause a decrease in the number of normal white blood corpuscles and blood platelets, and with the same results as mentioned earlier, the patient dies. Leukemia was well known even before our experiences with the atomic bomb and has long been recognized as a particularly lethal disease.

There are several other important questions concerning radiation that remain unanswered. Does radiation cause cataracts? Is there reason to fear that it may cause cancer? Is there a danger that deformities might appear in yet unborn children? The answers to these and other questions are uncertain, but the tenuous peace of mind that atomic bomb victims struggle to preserve can be disturbed by the mere mention of these issues. The medical profession is still in a state of confusion and can only state its uncertainty and apprehension whether some physical effects may persist years after the event. But if one were to tell atomic bomb victims, who have no technical medical knowledge, "We don't know what might happen to you next," what anxiety and desolation this would cause them! If it were an established fact that a certain symptom will invariably occur at some point, we would, of course, have to tell the patient, but at present we have no proof whatsoever either way. No clear evidence has yet emerged to connect radiation with cancer or birth defects.

RESEARCH ON ATOMIC BOMB DISEASE

When penicillin was first introduced into Japan not long after the end of the war, researchers at universities and general hospitals (not only those involved in the clinical field but those doing basic research as well) emptied their purses of what little money they had to buy penicillin on the black market and vied with one another for the lead in research in this area. Even Japanese research on tuberculosis, which was said to be at the highest level in the world, soon receded into the background.

At that time, I had my doubts about why the medical world should show so much interest in tuberculosis and surprisingly little in atomic bomb injury, which Japan alone of all the countries of the world had directly experienced. With the passage of time, my doubts gradually took definite shape: because atomic bomb injury far exceeds the imagination, it has been pushed aside as something remote and baffling by everyone except those who have actually experienced its effects and those immediately concerned with them.

That does not mean, however, that research on atomic bomb injury has been totally neglected. A few dedicated scientists have collected data on it even at the cost of their lives. This research began with the medical treatments attempted right after the bombings of Hiroshima and Nagasaki. But it took several months before organized research could make any headway on a systematic, scholarly basis. It is truly inspiring testimony to the dedicated efforts of scientists from the various universities and elsewhere that they were able to build the necessary organizations for this research at a time when all national functions had completely broken down. Advances were made steadily in all spheres of research related to atomic bomb injury.

Soon afterward, with the advent of the occupation period, members of a fact-finding mission from the United States joined these Japanese scientists, and together they were able to forward the work in many areas. Investigations on all fronts continued, as the United States formed the Atomic Bomb Casualty Commission (or ABCC, as it was commonly called, with administrative headquarters in Tokyo) and firmly established a research agenda. Meanwhile, the Japanese government set up a research organization as a special branch of the Society for the Promotion of Science.

Though the two commissions carry out their work very diligently, in at least one respect they are very different from normal scientific research institutes. Namely, both the United States and Japan are quite nervous about the publication of their findings. As long as this situation continues and those who have made specialized studies do not publish clear-cut findings, the ordinary citizen will never have any true understanding of atomic bomb injury. All the data sent by the ABCC to the United States are locked up somewhere, and only a few technical reports can be seen in scientific journals. At any rate in the United States today it is quite difficult for the American people to learn the scientific truth about atomic bomb casualties.

Recently the editorial staff of the magazine *Shizen* showed me an article in the September 1952 issue of the U.S. scientific journal *Nucleonics*. This article, called "Delayed Radiation Effects at Hiroshima and Nagasaki," by John C. Bugher, is a systematic report of the medical data but, unfortunately, it offers no explanation whatsoever about specific clinical problems.

In the past few years, science has become involved in some truly incomprehensible politics. Isn't it about time for science to resume its true form and pursue its true ends, investigating with thoroughness and detachment each and every phenomenon, recording its findings, and making these findings known? Since the atomic bomb is a colossal disaster produced by science, it is an especially distasteful subject for scientists to confront, but that makes unflinching observation and regulation all the more necessary.

Scientific development should advance and expand without limit. Every piece of data, no matter how trivial or silly it may seem, is in fact precious. Even research problems that are purely theoretical provide significant data. Those lazy souls who say they do not understand the goals of science or the direction it is moving in are merely parroting the nonsense of charlatans. This may have been accepted by a corrupt society of long ago, but it cannot be tolerated today.

To argue once again the pros and cons of making the atomic bomb is truly ridiculous. The proper path for science is to research further the energy which the atom holds. To employ this energy in the form of an explosive for wartime purposes is a misdirection of science. The people involved in building the bomb are surely aware of this fact, but their heads are full of war instead of ways to improve human life.

One often hears that war provides impetus to scientific development. Certainly, the massive mobilization of scientific talent and the successful completion of the atomic bomb was speeded up because of the war, and the science of nuclear energy, long only a dream of the human race, made rapid developments as a result of it. But, looked at in another way, it is the fact that war is a terrible crisis of humanity that necessitates the mobilization of talents of all kinds with great urgency. In times of peace, this sort of thing simply does not happen.

In other words, though we may say that war provides impetus to scientific development, what in fact we mean is that the large-scale mobilization of people who are dedicated to winning the war at all costs is what gives the impetus to that development. If so vast a mobilization of dedicated talents could take place in peacetime as well, the results would clearly be far more wonderful.

If we truly fear being involved in another war, the best method is not to play up atomic bomb damage or try to exploit it but to spread to the four corners of the earth as much accurate information about it as possible. Confronted with indisputable scientific facts, even the most wrong-thinking political power should amend its ways.

Radiation Sickness:
The Incurable Disease

Kobe Shimbun (The Kobe News)
April 18, 1954

Imagine that a patient enters a hospital complaining
that he does not feel well. As far as the patient is concerned, the purpose of this visit is, in effect, to be
relieved of both his present ill health and his fears for
the future. His doctor's task is to perform various tests
to determine the nature of the disease that has caused
the patient's condition. Once a diagnosis has been
made on the basis of these tests, the doctor can then
proceed to treat the ailment.

In addition to rendering such immediate benefits,
medical science's important functions include research
into various problems concerning the anatomy and
physiology of the human body and the search for the
underlying causes of disease. In other words, it is
the purpose of medical science to discover ways to
eliminate diseased conditions and restore health and
normality by understanding the functions of a normal
body and by studying the actual state of the disease.

To accomplish this end, medicine makes use of all

the achievements of science. There are, however, still many, many problems which remain unsolved, and, in certain cases, medical science would have been at a total loss for a cure if some new procedure had not been found. It was at just such a point that nuclear physics made its appearance.

The very mention of nuclear energy is likely to stir up feelings of horror and revulsion because it immediately brings to mind nuclear weapons, which have recently once again become a major cause for concern. But these feelings are due to the fact that nuclear energy was abused when it was first employed as an instrument of war. The essential nature of nuclear physics might actually be considered the fulfillment of man's dreams. Just as a knife, for example, can be the cause of human happiness or human suffering depending on its use, nuclear physics, if properly used, promises an extremely prosperous future. Research into the uses of atomic energy as a power source is already well under way, and it has become indispensable for research carried on in various basic sciences. As a result of important research methods developed in the fields of agriculture and biology in general, atomic energy has provided an absolutely indispensable tool for medical research and therapy.

This tool is the use of radioisotopes. By implanting into the human body matter artificially treated with radioactivity and by studying into which parts of the body most of these isotopes enter, it is possible to learn more about the body's physiological functions. In like manner, it has become possible to make a localized diagnosis of a malignant tumor, which will absorb only a certain kind of matter. By irradiating an isotope and then searching for it with a geiger counter, we can discover which elements behave in what ways within the human body. Radioisotopes used in this fashion are known as tracers. These tracers can be followed not only externally with the help of a geiger counter but internally as well. A radio autograph can be made by capturing on a special type of film the radioactive tracer that has been absorbed by the cells and tissues of the body, allowing very detailed research into how this radioactive matter is distributed throughout the body.

By such use of radioisotopes—irradiating matter to be purposely absorbed where there is a particular morbid condition (mainly malignant tumors) and then inserting this in the body—it is possible to treat conditions that do not fully respond to X-ray or radium therapy. In addition, in the future, the various byproducts of atomic science and industry will make possible great strides in areas related to medical science, such as food preservation.

If, however, atomic energy is used to kill people, we must evaluate it in a different way. There is nothing within the power of modern medicine that can be done to combat its effects. It might be thought that medical science has made such great progress that it should somehow be able to cure all the injuries inflicted by nuclear explosions, but, in fact, it cannot. If a nuclear weapon were to be dropped on a city somewhere, not only would all the buildings in the area of impact be demolished by the force of the blast and the intense heat, but most of the people living there would be killed instantly. Of those who managed to escape immediate death, the number of injured in need of medical treatment would be too great for the medical facilities to handle, assuming, of course, that such facilities had themselves survived the bombing and were still functioning. These facilities, however, like all others in the city, would be totally demolished. And, on top of all this, the survivors would be exposed to radiation sickness, incurable by modern medicine.

Today, specialists not only in Japan but throughout the world are making efforts to discover some method to remove or neutralize radioactivity once it has penetrated the human body. So far, however, no such method has been found. Research and therapy that make use of the radioisotopes mentioned earlier use the minimum dosage of radioactivity necessary for each specific purpose, and its effects soon disappear. But it is impossible to prescribe limits to the radioactivity produced by the atomic bomb. A human body exposed to large quantities of radiation that does not disappear no matter how many years pass is gradually eroded by a terrifying and invisible destructive force.

There is no sense debating the pros and cons of nuclear physics. The sciences developed by man will continue to make greater and greater progress. But something can and must be done about the thought processes of man himself, who decides to what ends nuclear physics will be used.

AS AUGUST 9TH
COMES ROUND AGAIN

A Last Letter from
Chief Orderly Iyonaga

In the summer of 1977, I received a letter from former chief orderly Yasumasa Iyonaga, who figured so prominently in the first part of this book. An eyewitness to horrors which defy description, he had been dispatched to Nagasaki right after the bomb fell, and, on his return to Omura, had been involved in caring for the bomb victims in the ward under my command. He now lives a peaceful life as an ordinary civilian with no involvement with either the military or the atomic bomb. But how has this ordinary citizen borne the burden of that horrifying experience during the past thirty-odd years? How vividly is that experience incised in his memory even today? This letter of his relates more eloquently than anything else the situation since then.

In addition to a tendency to cast me in too favorable a light, there are places in this letter which show how even the most horrible experiences can weather into fond memories with the passage of more than thirty years. For that reason, I was slightly hesitant about including the entire text of the letter here. On the other hand, it was this letter that stimulated me to write my own account of these events, and so with Iyonaga's permission, I have presumed to include it.

"Dear Dr. Shiotsuki:

"Summer with its sweltering heat has finally arrived. I hope this letter finds you in good health. Although thirty-two years have slipped by since the atomic bombing of Nagasaki, the coming of the burning summer weather invariably revives in my mind memories of that fateful moment and what those days were like, as though it were only yesterday.

"On that day, I had gone to disinfect a small island in Omura Bay. I shall never forget that instant of intense brightness, the terrific blast, and the lurid-colored atomic cloud, curling like long tongues of fire in the sky above Nagasaki, then drifting off slowly, borne along by the wind. Soon afterwards, I was called back from the island and made a member of the hastily organized the Omura Naval Hospital Special Relief Mission under Lieutenant Jinnai. We took off on a bus filled with medical supplies for the scene of the bombing, still rawly enveloped in tragedy. What a pitiful sight the people of Nagasaki presented to us during the more than twenty hours we spent there, working without rest to give first aid to the victims.

"When I returned to Omura, I found Ward 8 filled to overflowing with atomic bomb victims and throngs of the critically injured setting out one after another on life's final journey. Among the dying, Tsuru Kurita and her daughter Hideko, who both passed away on August 12, were so pitiful that I could not even look at them without tears welling up in my eyes. Tsuru Kurita had received injuries from the bomb while she had been bending over weeding in the field of her home in Nishimachi, Nishiurakami. The upper half of her body had been exposed at the time of the blast, and she was admitted to the hospital with critical burns on her back, neck, and both arms. The burns were so severe that bacillus pyocyaneus (a discharge of greenish pus, the most dreaded and difficult to treat infection occurring in external injuries) had set in, and maggots had begun to breed in the pus. She lay there on the verge of death, face down, unable to move, moaning in agony.

"In the bed next to her, her thirteen-year-old daughter Hideko lay close to death with burns on her face and over her entire body. The two of them had been admitted to the hospital separately but had been recognized as mother and daughter because of their identical surnames and placed in adjoining beds. Unable even to hold each other's hands, they would call out words of encouragement to one another in feeble voices. How tragic was the sight of that mother, herself in critical condition, unable to do a thing as her daughter passed away right before her very eyes. I was there looking on at this pitiful scene and could not move away. Several hours after Hideko had died, Tsuru thanked me for taking care of her daughter, then she too breathed her last.

"The death of Toshie Yamashita, eighteen, from Fujitsu in Saga Prefecture, is also indelibly engraved in my memory. I heard that she had a lovely voice and often sang on the Nagasaki radio station. You had surgically removed the glass fragments from her thigh; her condition had improved; and she was looking forward to being released soon from the hospital when suddenly the symptoms of radiation disease began to appear, and her condition deteriorated with each succeeding day. Her father rushed in from her hometown to help care for her. When the end was near, she asked him to help her put on clean underwear and a fresh *yukata,* then she combed her hair, lightly applied some makeup, and peacefully passed away. The sight of that father and daughter deeply struck everyone.

"I suppose it was about the third day after the bomb fell that I noticed a lot of hair on the pillow on Toshio Omune's bed, which was the first one on the right just as you entered the ward. I thought he had had his hair cut, and when I looked at his head it was closely though unevenly cropped. 'It's all right to cut your hair, Omune,' I said, 'but not in bed. It's been pretty carelessly done, though. Who in the world cut it for you?' He looked very puzzled and replied in dead earnest, 'I didn't have my hair cut. It shouldn't be short.' I patted his head to give him some idea what it was now like, but as soon as I touched his hair, it fell out in great quantities with no resistance whatsoever. Realizing that this must be the symptom of some serious illness, I immediately had a blood cell count and several other tests taken.

"Then I went into another room and found Medical Corpsman First Class Segawa in a heated exchange with Yukie Ezaki, who must have been about twenty or so. Yukie had asked for a drink of water, but Segawa had told her to wait awhile because she had just had one and drinking too much was not good for her. I went up to her bed and told her that she would wear herself out talking in such a loud voice and to speak more quietly. As I said this, I put my hand on her head and gently stroked her hair. Immediately dozens of the strands of black hair I had touched fell out. I was startled, but since it is forbidden to show any expression of surprise in front of a patient, I said nothing but surreptitiously tried pulling at her hair. Just as in the case of Omune, it came out with no resistance.

"Then I asked her to show me her arm and was surprised to see that symptoms of purpura had begun to appear there. In addition, she showed signs of minor bleeding from the gums. I hurried back to Omune and, as expected, there were also spots on his body and hemorrhaging from his gums. A half year earlier, Yanagawa, a fellow soldier about the same age as I, had died of purpura hemorrhagica. The symptoms I was now seeing before me were identical with what I had seen so often when I had visited Yanagawa's sickbed.

"Convinced beyond doubt in my own mind that these were cases of purpura hemorrhagica I reported the situation in detail to you. You listened to my report, thought about it for a while, then immediately said, 'I don't believe that these are simple cases of pur-pura hemorrhagica. Please check the condition of all the other patients right away.' After a thorough check of everyone in Ward 8, three or four more patients were discovered to be suffering from these same symp-toms. I reported these results back to you, and you told me to report the situation immediately to the head of the hospital. 'This is a serious discovery,' you told me, 'You may be the first person at Omura Naval Hospital to detect symptoms caused by the "special bomb".'

"I did not understand what you were talking about, but I reported immediately to the director of the hospital. He too was very surprised and alarmed and immediately ordered me to examine all the bomb vic-tims in the entire hospital for these symptoms. As or-dered, I hurried around from ward to ward in the vast hospital complex, examining each and every patient, and discovered more than fifty cases of loss of hair, more than twenty with an abnormal dark purplish pat-terning on their skin around the site of injections, and more than ten with symptoms of purpura and hemor-rhaging from the gums. Of this last group, the great majority were in critical condition.

"Up to that point we had watched helplessly as the victims of burns and other external injuries had lapsed into critical condition. Now the situation completely changed. Epilation and symptoms of purpura occurred in patients regardless of whether their burns or wounds were serious or not and even in those seemingly well on the road to recovery. If bleeding from the gums occurred as well, the patient invariably died. These radiation victims were all lucid right up to the very end and could speak clearly though very feebly. They approached their deaths with extreme reluctance. The sight of these pitiful, helpless people was tragic beyond description, and even if I tried, I could never forget them as long as I live.

"As I recall, it was just about one month before the bomb fell that you and I first met. I was a twenty-five-year-old draftee, a chief medical corpsman in the navy. You came to Omura as a doctor in training and were assigned to Ward 8, where I was serving as senior orderly. In a short time, we had overcome the barriers imposed by the difference in our respective ranks and positions and became good friends, even taking our leaves together on several occasions. And then just as we were making preparations to receive casualties from the anticipated invasion of the Japanese mainland, what should suddenly burst upon us but the tragedy of the atomic bomb.

"In the midst of all that horror and chaos, your actions as a doctor and as a scientist turned completely inside out all the preconceptions I had had about doctors from the physicians and army doctors I had hitherto known. I remember your reactions as patients, though seemingly not seriously injured, one after another lapsed into critical condition; as liquid from intravenous injections dripped out of their veins though the needles had been properly inserted; as they lost the power to absorb even a hypodermic injection; as one by one they took a turn for the worse, weakened, and died, though they remained lucid until the very end.

"I knew I was trapped when you turned to me and said, 'This is a terrible situation. I must find out why this is happening right away. First, I have to investigate the causes, then make permanent records of the findings. But I cannot do it alone. Please help me.' The extreme seriousness with which you said these words and the expression in your eyes have always remained in my mind.

"What we did then, of course, was the autopsies of bomb victims. Though I have absolutely no technical knowledge of medicine, I still remember your surprise and even your very words during that very first autopsy in the room behind the mortuary—'Hemorrhaging as far as the mesentery; veins in shreds; liver not functioning at all.' After that first autopsy, I helped you do dozens more and made copies of your clinical reports. But I could only steal a few moments from my hectic rounds nursing the living and was not able to give you all the help you needed.

"Recently I was able to find the names and addresses of three of the nurses who worked in Ward 8— Mitsue Kobayashi, Masae Yamaji, Mumeno Fujisawa, as well as that of Osamu Segawa, an orderly about my age—and to talk with them on the telephone. All of them helped you with the care of patients, with your autopsies, and with copying your clinical reports. They all remember you well. And one of them even sent a snapshot of those of us from Ward 8, taken after the war on the day before we were discharged from the navy. All three of the nurses and

Medical Corpsman First Class Segawa are in the picture.

"Memories overwhelm me as I look at this snapshot. But of all the countless memories I have of those times, none has made a deeper impression on me than your actions and attitude in the midst of all that chaos, both as a scientist and as a doctor entrusted with the care of human life. Though we have both gone our separate ways, it is impossible for me to measure the extent to which your behavior in those days has influenced my life since then: your impassioned dedication to research and to medical care, your weighty sense of responsibility to the future of society, to say nothing of your consideration for your patients as a doctor and your lofty spirit of humanism as a man.

"I started writing this letter intending merely to inquire after your health during the hot season and to jot down a simple account of some memories we shared together. But one memory after another has been reawakened in the process, and this has turned into a very long letter, and, I am afraid, quite a confused and rambling one at that.

"I sincerely hope that you will spend the summer in good health. Please take good care of yourself and please convey my very best wishes to your wife.

"With vivid memories of that summer thirty-two years ago and my sincere best wishes for your health during the present hot weather, I remain sincerely yours,

Yasumasa Iyonaga
August 9, 1977''